SWEDEN

SWEDEN

Titles in the Modern Nations of the World series include:

Brazil
Canada
China
Cuba
Egypt
England
Germany
Greece
India
Ireland
Italy
Japan
Kenya
Mexico
Russia
Somalia
South Africa
South Korea
Spain
Sweden
The United States

SWEDEN

BY LESLEY A. DUTEMPLE

LUCENT BOOKS
P.O. BOX 289011
SAN DIEGO, CA 92198-9011

Library of Congress Cataloging-in-Publication Data

DuTemple, Lesley A.
    Sweden / by Lesley A. DuTemple.
        p.   cm. — (Modern nations of the world)
    Includes bibliographical references and index.
    Summary: Examines the land, people, history, and culture of Sweden
and discusses its current state of affairs and place in the world today.
    ISBN 1-56006-588-5 (lib. bdg. : alk. paper)
    1. Sweden—Juvenile literature. [1. Sweden.] I. Title.   II. Series.
DL609.D85 2000
948.5—dc21
                                                                        99-30142
                                                                          CIP

Copyright © 2000 by Lucent Books, Inc.
P.O. Box 289011, San Diego, CA 92198-9011
Printed in the U.S.A.

CONTENTS

INTRODUCTION

THOROUGHLY MODERN, WITH ROOTS IN THE PAST

Every nation has a history, but few have managed to incorporate their past as thoroughly into their present-day existence as Sweden. In a land of rich geographical diversity, ancient Viking rune stones coexist next to modern highway markers.

Since its emergence from prehistoric glaciers, Sweden's rich history has played a vital role in the nation's modern-day existence. The blueprint for Sweden's Riksdag, or parliament, can be traced back to the 800s. Although adapted to accommodate Sweden's growing population and place in the global community, the original concept of the Riksdag has changed very little over the centuries.

Likewise, present-day Swedes embody many of the principles their ancestors held dear: namely, a concept of individual freedom, fairness for all, and a commitment to community. Even the Viking love of the sea, nature, fine design, and quality craftsmanship has been carried through the ages.

But for all of the reminders of the past that are found in Sweden, it is a thoroughly modern country. Sweden is one of the most technologically advanced countries in the world. For decades its population has also enjoyed one of the highest standards of living in the world, with a highly educated populace and virtually no poverty. Sweden is also one of the world's cleanest countries since it is likewise committed to the environment. Its industrial and technological growth has been fueled primarily by hydroelectric power—one of the cleanest power sources available.

Many people consider Sweden the embodiment of intellectual excellence and humanitarian ideals, and as a nation, Sweden enjoys the respect of the international community. Education has been compulsory for more than 150 years, and Sweden's literacy rate is nearly 100 percent. And for many, the coveted Nobel Prizes (awarded annually for intellectual and peacekeeping achievements) epitomize the country's pursuit of intellectual excellence. As for humanitarian ideals, Sweden has progressed far from its origins in Viking violence. Since the late 1700s, Sweden has maintained a policy of military neutrality, meaning the country has refused to take sides in any war. Sweden even remained neutral during both World Wars, although the Swedes aided refugees from Nazi Germany during World War II.

Sweden's military neutrality goes hand in hand with a commitment to world peace. In keeping with this commitment, Sweden has been active in the United Nations (an

This nineteenth-century ship, a symbol of Sweden's seafaring past, stands next to a modern symbol of the country's advanced technology, an IBM building.

international organization of countries devoted to the peaceful solution of conflicts around the world) since the organization's founding. The country has also participated in nearly every peacekeeping mission in which the United Nations has engaged.

Swedes are proud of both their progressive modern culture and their Viking heritage. The people of Sweden have not always been peaceful, but they have always been committed to the ideals of equality among individuals as well as what is best for the community as a whole. As a nation, Sweden's past coexists peacefully with its present and continues to influence and shape its future.

A Land of Contrasts

Sweden is a land of contrasts. The fourth-largest country in Europe, Sweden is approximately 980 miles long (1,575 kilometers) and 310 miles wide (500 kilometers). It is just a little larger than the state of California. Yet within these nearly 1,000 miles lies some of the earth's most varied terrain. Sweden encompasses icy glaciers, fertile plains, rushing rivers, sandy beaches, peat bogs, and vast forests. Approximately 68 percent of the country is covered with forest and woodland. Nearly one hundred thousand lakes dot its surface.

Sweden is located high atop the earth's northern pole. The northern part of Sweden lies within the Arctic Circle, and for much of the year, snow and ice blanket the land. At the North Pole, nothing is moderate—even the pattern of sunlight is extreme. Summer is only a couple of months long, but during those months the sun never sets. Wildflowers burst into bloom and grow continuously in the constant sunlight. The entire growing season for the Arctic Circle is packed into approximately eight weeks. But winter is the opposite. For months at a time, the sun never rises above the horizon, and all is dark and frozen.

Only one thousand miles away, the southern part of Sweden is a land of mild temperatures, fertile farmland, and blooming fruit orchards. Southern Sweden experiences the benefits of the North Atlantic Current. This current of warm water sweeps across the Atlantic, mingling with and warming the waters of the North and Baltic Seas. The warm water produces a much milder climate than would typically be experienced for such a northern country, for even the southern reaches of Sweden are still very far north of the equator. Although there is plenty of snow during the winter, the snow does not usually arrive until November, and throughout the winter the temperature usually does not drop below 20 degrees Fahrenheit (–5 degrees Celsius). True cold snaps are rare, and spring usually arrives in April and May.

The eastern and western regions of Sweden are equally varied. In the west, the craggy Kölen Mountains run the northwestern length of the country, separating Sweden from Norway. Most Swedish rivers originate in the snowy peaks of the Kölen Mountains. Sweden's eastern boundary is the Baltic seacoast.

THE FORCE OF ANCIENT ICE

Sweden was not always a land of contrasts. Nearly fourteen thousand years ago the whole of present-day Sweden was covered by an enormous ice cap. Ice, many miles thick, stretched from the northern reaches of the Arctic Circle, across Sweden, and down to the southern regions that now border the Baltic and North Seas. Ice built up over hundreds of years, becoming so thick and heavy that it compressed the land. Even today, thousands of years after the ice melted, the land of Sweden is still rising, trying to spring back to its original elevation.

As the ice cap melted, individual glaciers remained in many parts of Sweden. The glaciers moved, scouring the earth's surface as they crept across the landscape. They smoothed out mountains and rock formations, created sandy ridges and depressions, and carved out valleys. When the remaining ice cap and glaciers finally melted, they left behind a huge lake that covered much of the land. With most of the ice gone, the land began to rise, creating the Kölen Mountains, and the glacial water drained off into the seas. A great deal of water remained behind, though. The depressions and furrows left by the scouring glaciers filled with water, creating nearly one hundred thousand lakes across Sweden.

THE SCANDINAVIAN COUNTRIES

Sweden is one of five Nordic, or Scandinavian, countries. The others are Norway, Denmark, Finland, and Iceland. Together, Sweden and Norway make up the Scandinavian Peninsula. Denmark was once connected to the peninsula; its shape fits right into the space between the southern tips of Sweden and Norway. All of the Scandinavian countries were shaped, in some way, by ice.

Ice is not the only thing that the five countries have in common. All five countries were originally populated by Germanic tribes, and at times the Scandinavian countries have also mingled their rulership: From 1814 until 1905 Norway was peacefully ruled by Sweden, and parts of Sweden have been under Danish rule. Over three hundred years ago, the southern part of Sweden was under Danish rule. Although the current inhabitants of that area are thoroughly Swedish, many of them speak a dialect of Swedish that has strong traces of Danish.

The majestic, jagged peak of Skierfe Mountain forms part of the Kölen Mountains, a chain created when the land rose after the retreat of the glaciers.

Since ancient times, the Scandinavian countries have often functioned as if they were a single nation. Today, this practice still holds true, primarily through the Nordic Council of Ministers.

Every year the leaders of the five countries meet to discuss possible solutions to common problems. Topics that come up during the annual meeting concern such matters as energy, education, environmental protection, industry, and trade.

Citizens of all five Scandinavian countries can move freely among the countries without passports or visas. They may also work in another Scandinavian country without obtaining a work permit. When living in another Scandinavian country, they are treated as citizens of that country and are entitled to the same benefits as native citizens. This tradition of cooperation and mingling between the different regions of Scandinavia has existed since the area was first settled at the close of the Ice Age.

EARLY INHABITANTS

The many thousands of lakes, including this one near Halmstad in southern Sweden, were formed when the melting ice cap filled depressions carved out by glaciers.

Sweden's ice cap took longer to melt than the ones covering southern European countries such as Germany and Italy. In the far north, at the Arctic Circle, the ice cap never entirely melted. Today, northern Sweden still remains the least-populated area of the country, and Lapland, in general, is one of the least-populated areas of the globe.

EVERYMAN'S RIGHT

In Sweden, there are no laws against walking on private or public lands. Everyone is free to swim, hike, or dock a boat wherever he or she likes without special permits or permission. People are free to help themselves to edible plants and berries in the woods and forests. This ancient tradition is called "Everyman's Right."

Along with the privilege of Everyman's Right, the Swedish people recognize the need to respect other people's property. Although Swedes are legally free to do so, they do not walk through other people's gardens and planted fields. They are also careful not to harm the environment by overpicking plants or by littering.

Inhospitable as snow and ice are, the first inhabitants of Sweden arrived while ice still covered much of the country. While the ice age that shaped Sweden ended about ten thousand years ago, scientific evidence indicates that the first people moved into the area about twelve thousand years ago. According to the Swedish Institute, "As the ice slowly retreated, man came to Sweden and the first known human dwelling place, which has been found in southern Sweden, dates from around 10,000 B.C."[1]

These first inhabitants came from the area that is now northern Germany. Because of geographic isolation, the Germanic origins of Sweden's population are evident even today. Most Scandinavian languages retain many similarities to the German language.

GÖTALAND: THE FERTILE SOUTH

Sweden can be divided into three geographic regions: southern Sweden, or Götaland; central and eastern Sweden, or Svealand; and northern Sweden, or Norrland.

Götaland was the first region of Sweden to emerge from the ice. Within Götaland, two different types of terrain exist: the lowlands of Skåne and the Småland Highlands.

Scientists think that the first humans in Scandinavia settled in Skåne. The fertile valleys and flat coastal plains—both rich with minerals and deposits left by retreating glaciers—are ideal for farming. Today, Skåne is Sweden's top agricultural region.

SWEDEN'S NATIONAL PARK SYSTEM

In 1909 Sweden established the first national park system in Europe. Today, there are twenty national parks in Sweden, ranging from tiny recreational areas in the south to vast wilderness preserves in the northern mountains.

Sweden's national park system was designed to protect both its natural environment and its cultural history. One of the parks, Sanfjället, is a thick forest primarily inhabited by bears. Other parks honor the sites of legendary giants and trolls.

Sixteen of the twenty parks are located in Norrland, and of those sixteen, six are located above the Arctic Circle in Lapland.

Sweden's national park system has assured that large quantities of wilderness and natural landscape are preserved yet available for people to enjoy.

North of Skåne lies the Småland Highlands. Småland is an area mostly located on Sweden's southeastern seacoast. Småland has a rocky, irregular coastline composed of numerous bays, inlets, sandy beaches, and white cliffs. Thousands of islands lie just offshore.

Småland has a cooler, wetter climate than Skåne, and its soil does not support the rich variety of agriculture that Skåne's does. The northern part of Småland is hilly and slopes steeply down to plains. Peat bogs and clay deposits can be found throughout the landscape. Småland is also more heavily wooded than Skåne—nearly two-thirds of the region is covered with deciduous (leafy) and coniferous (cone-producing) trees. Forestry is a major industry in Småland, although agricultural farms are also very important.

SVEALAND

North of Småland is Svealand, the central and eastern coastal region of Sweden. *Svealand* means "land of the Swedes," and it has lakes, plains, and rolling hills. The Svealand region slopes eastward from a plateau on the western edge of Sweden to a narrow coastal plain along the Baltic Sea. Although considered central Sweden, Svealand actually lies in the southern part of the country.

Although the climate of central Sweden is mild, it is wetter than Götaland. In addition to the seacoast, Svealand also has many lakes. Fishing is an important industry in Svealand, as is agriculture.

Most of Sweden's mineral resources are located in Svealand. During the seventeenth and eighteenth centuries, a large copper mine in Falun produced two-thirds of the world's copper ore. Although the mine is no longer actively producing large amounts of copper, copper from the region can still be seen all over Sweden: The red paint used on so many homes contains Falun copper. More than three hundred different minerals are also in the region, although most of them are not plentiful enough to merit mining.

Stockholm, the nation's capital and largest city, is located in Svealand. Situated between the seacoast and Lake Mälaren, Stockholm is built on fourteen different islands. More than twenty-four thousand small islands ring the city and are referred to as "Stockholm's pearl necklace." Although few people inhabit these islands on a year-round basis, many keep vacation homes there.

One of the fourteen islands that make up Stockholm, Sweden's capital and largest city.

THE FROZEN NORTH

North of Svealand, reaching all the way to Sweden's northern border, is Norrland. Norrland comprises three-fifths of Sweden's land. Although it is Sweden's largest region, Norrland is the least-populated area of the country.

Norrland contains rocky mountain peaks, rolling hills, high plateaus, and broad river valleys. Its eastern border slopes into a narrow coastal plain along the Gulf of Bothnia in the Baltic Sea. Most of the region is heavily forested, and aside from the river valleys, the soil is poor and unsuited for farming. In western Norrland, much of the land is located above the timberline, the elevation where trees will grow.

Sweden's nickname, "the Land of the Midnight Sun," comes from a Norrland phenomenon. During the summer, the sun does not set over Norrland for two months. But Norrland

A snow-covered landscape in the Swedish part of Lapland, which stretches across the northernmost parts of Norway, Sweden, Finland, and Russia.

could also be referred to as "the Land of Eternal Midnight," as the sun does not rise for two months during midwinter.

In many ways, Norrland is like a country in and of itself because it is the portion of Sweden that is part of Lapland. Lapland recognizes no distinct borders, but rather refers to the northernmost portions of Norway, Sweden, Finland, and Russia. There, the indigenous people of the region, the Sami, move freely about the area, with little regard for political borders.

The Sami inhabited the area of northern Sweden long before Germanic tribes moved into southern Sweden. But whereas scientists can trace the development of Sweden's population as it moved northward from the European mainland, the origins of the Sami are uncertain. Today, about sixty thousand Sami live in the region known as Lapland. Of this total, about seventeen thousand Sami live in Sweden.

DIVERSE LANDSCAPE, DIVERSE WILDLIFE

Given its diverse landscape and sparse population pattern, Sweden has one of the richest concentrations of wildlife in all of Europe. With an average of only fifty-one people per square mile (twenty per square kilometer), there is plenty of room for wildlife habitat in Sweden.

Sweden boasts the longest coastline in Europe (stretching approximately 4,600 miles long, or 7,600 kilometers) and, consequently, some of the best fishing in the world. Large salmon and trout inhabit the coastal waters, lakes, and rivers.

In addition to an abundance of aquatic life, bears, lynx, Arctic foxes, and other animals inhabit the forests. There are also about 40 wolves living in the country, which are protected by law. Still, Sweden is really the land of the moose. With a population of 250,000, spread from the north to the southern regions, Sweden has the highest density of moose in the world.

Hunting is an established tradition in Sweden, and moose are only one of several animals that are hunted. Bears, deer, foxes, grouse, and others all have set hunting seasons every year.

POPULATING A DIVERSE LANDSCAPE

By 6000 B.C. all of Sweden was inhabited, from the farms of Götaland to the frozen reaches of Norrland.

CAROLUS LINNAEUS

By the mid-1700s naturalists were beginning to recognize the need to classify and categorize the world's various plant and animal species.

A young Swedish student named Carl von Linné was particularly interested in categorizing the natural world, and after much thought, he created a filing system that is still used today.

First, he looked at all living organisms and assigned those that were similar to one of several *classes*. Within each class, the organisms were assigned to *orders* based on further similarities. Then each order was further broken down into *genera*, then finally into *species*. The most important thing that von Linné did was to assign a unique scientific name—in Latin—to each organism, identifying its genus and species in descriptive terms. Common names differ around the world, but von Linné's scientific name remains the same.

Carl von Linné even went so far as to assign himself a scientific name: Carolus Linnaeus, which is how the world knows him.

Carolus Linnaeus created a system of classifying all living organisms.

Despite its geographical isolation from the European continent, Scandinavia was known throughout Europe. Pliny the Elder, a civil servant in the Roman Empire, wrote about Sweden as early as A.D. 79. Sweden's Luleå University reports that, in his encyclopedia *Historia naturalis,* Pliny writes

> about an Island in the north called Scandinavia, populated by "illa suionum gente" which according to him lives in 500 villages scattered over the island. The name is debatable, but some do think that he means "sveonerna" or [Swedish] people. If that's the case then this would be the first written document which says something about Sweden in its early time.[2]

And in A.D. 120, the Egyptian geographer Ptolemy created the first map on which Sweden was actually shown.

The people of the Scandinavian region might have continued to develop in quiet isolation were it not for their seafaring skills. Around the year 800, they took to the seas and aggressively made their mark on the world. Within only a few years, they were known—and feared—throughout the world. The age of the Vikings had arrived.

A Rich and Diverse History

Around the year 800, archaeologists believe that Scandinavia may have faced extreme overpopulation. Although the land in the southern regions was fertile, there was not enough of it to grow the crops necessary to feed a burgeoning population. To the north, forests and mountains dominated the landscape. People logged and herded in these regions, but it was difficult to grow food. At that time only about 9 percent of Sweden's land was good for farming, and most people had to be fishermen as well as farmers and herders in order to survive. With agricultural land in such short supply, many Scandinavians ventured forth to set up new colonies and began raiding other areas, including Russia, Iceland, Greenland, France, and the British Isles.

As the Scandinavians moved into lands that were already populated, they became known as the Vikings, a name derived from an Old English word meaning "pirate." To the Europeans, any Scandinavian who went raiding was a Viking. Today, however, the word *Viking* is often used to describe any Scandinavian person who lived during the years 800 to 1100.

Mastering the Art of Shipbuilding

It was the Vikings' shipbuilding skills that made it possible for them to cross oceans and raid other countries. While people from other coastal regions struggled to construct seaworthy vessels, the people of Scandinavia mastered the art of building large ships that were both fast and seaworthy. These ships were called longships, and they were built with keels. A keel is a long piece of wood that extends the length of the boat—on the exterior bottom side—to keep the boat stable and help prevent it from tipping over. Nowadays many boats are built with keels, but in the 800s it was a new idea.

According to an article in *Scientific American,* "The long-ship's perfect mating of design, structure and material derives neither from a single creative genius nor even a single age. Rather these vessels represent the culmination of 6,000 years of technical evolution."[3]

Longships were powered by rowing with oars and also by using large square sails that caught the wind and gave them added speed. The ships were fast. In fact, in 1893 a group of researchers constructed one and sailed from Bergen, Norway, to Newfoundland. They reached the North American continent in only twenty-eight days. And in 1962, two longships were discovered in a sea channel off Denmark. The boats had been deliberately sunk by townspeople to serve as barricades against raiders. But according to *Scientific American,* "Both ships in fact showed many seasons of wear, evidence that longships were more seaworthy than some scholars had thought."[4] Longships were also silent. Frequently, the ships were beached and the men were ashore before their intended victims could sound warnings.

The Vikings may have begun raiding other lands as a result of overpopulation and limited resources at home.

NORTHERN PIRATES

In 793 the Vikings launched a surprise raid on the Lindisfarne Monastery, marking the beginning of the Viking age. Striking swiftly and mercilessly, they plundered the monastery and killed the monks. According to author Eric Oxenstierna, "Lindisfarne, on the border between England and Scotland, was a place of such sanctity that the indignation of the Christian world was doubly great."[5]

For the next few hundred years, the Vikings wreaked havoc on the European continent and the British Isles. As Oxenstierna points out, even powerful rulers had to deal with them: "Charlemagne found even his coronation year overshadowed, as he hastened to Friesland to institute a coastal watch. Despite the Emperor's precautions the [Vikings] continued to batter at these inhospitable shores."[6]

People have typically remembered the Vikings as ruthless, cold-blooded killers. But while they were certainly violent raiders, they were also colonizers and traders. Their initial forays into other countries were likely prompted by reasons

The longships' combination of speed, silence, and strength allowed the Vikings to overpower their neighbors and raid at will.

THE SWEDISH VIKINGS

Although most early Scandinavians spoke the same language and Europeans considered them all to be Norsemen, historians now note that there were differences between the Vikings.

The Danish and Norwegian Vikings went westward in their expeditions, concentrating on western Europe and England. The Swedish Vikings ventured eastward into modern-day Russia. The Swedish Vikings also traveled farther eastward than any other European people, even going as far as Jerusalem, Baghdad, and the Caspian Sea.

Another difference between the two groups was that the Danish and Norwegian Vikings tended to conquer and colonize, whereas the Swedish Vikings traded. Although the Swedes were certainly well-armed fighting men, they usually did not seek to establish kingdoms or colonies.

other than a desire to plunder and terrorize. According to Oxenstierna, people used to think that "each successful foray, . . . only stimulated the black-hearted pagans to further wickedness. . . . [But] modern scholarship has suggested an entirely different set of motives. . . . The main reason stares us in the face: overpopulation."[7] Around the ninth century, the population in Sweden appears to have burgeoned, yet the amount of land then available for farming did not increase.

Although many scholars believe the main reason for raiding was overpopulation in their homelands, still others argue that the traditional inheritance laws figured prominently into the reasons for raiding. When Viking families had more than one son, the oldest son inherited everything upon the death of his parents, and the younger sons were left to fend for themselves. Raiding and claiming territory in other lands, then, was one way younger sons were able to acquire a home and farmland for themselves.

A SOPHISTICATED SOCIETY

There is no doubt that the Vikings could be cruel and merciless invaders, but only strong and relatively young freemen, known as *karls,* went on raids. Women, children, and older people stayed home and tended the agricultural settlements

This detailed band worn around the upper arm is typical of the intricate jewelry designed and crafted by the Vikings.

that were the real backbone of Viking society. And although their violence is well documented, even raiding parties only operated when the weather was fair enough for sea voyages—usually in late spring through early autumn. The rest of the year the Vikings stayed close to home working as farmers, shipbuilders, weavers, and artisans. They are credited with developing a written language, opening trade centers, and establishing a democratic form of government. The Vikings were also an artistic society, fashioning fine jewelry and utensils and weaving beautiful, colorful cloth.

The Vikings appear to have been shrewd, successful businessmen as well. In 830 they founded the city of Dublin, Ireland, and by 850 they had established trading centers in Russia and the Baltic region. In fact, the Russian city of Kiev, which became a major trading center, was founded by Swedish merchants. There, the Vikings were known as the "Rus"—after which Russia is named. In 874 the Vikings established a settlement in Iceland, and by 900 most Viking traveling was done primarily to establish trading settlements.

The first towns in Sweden also started as trading centers, places where goods could be sold or exchanged peaceably. Birka, located on an island in Lake Mälaren, near present-day Stockholm, was the main trading center. Birka was a large town of about fifty thousand people, and because the town was surrounded by rivers and lakes, goods could easily be transported to and from the surrounding regions. Archaeological work has established that the town was surrounded by a protective wall made of dirt and wood. Archaeologists also know that approximately two thousand inhabitants served and protected the town, much like modern-day police officers.

Activity in the town inexplicably came to an abrupt end at the close of the ninth century. Today, Birka is an important archaeological site, with several Scandinavian universities and organizations participating in the excavation. The site has yielded jewelry and pottery from foreign lands as well as Arabic coins. More than eighty-five thousand such coins have been found throughout Scandinavia. Because the coins are dated and can be traced to their country of origin, researchers know where and when the Vikings traveled.

THE STORY IN STONE

The ancient Vikings spoke a language called Old Norse. It was based on two sixteen-rune alphabets called futharks. A rune is a figure or symbol. The alphabets are named after the first six letters—which spell the word futhark. The Vikings used these runes to form words and sentences, which can still be deciphered and read today.

Lacking paper and pen, the Vikings carved runes into stones and wood. Rune stones were carved and erected to mark graves and bridges, and many can still be found throughout Scandinavia and other parts of Europe.

In Iceland, the modern population speaks a language almost identical to the early Viking language. Even English contains many words that originate from the Vikings. The English word *by* is Viking for "town." In England, the place name *Danby* is Viking for "Dane Town," and the word *bylaw* means "the law of the town." Other words, such as *die, them,* and *take,* are also of Viking origin.

In fact, most of what is known about the Vikings comes from archaeological excavations throughout Scandinavia and Europe. These excavations, along with information contained in rune stones, have yielded glimpses into a complex and well-ordered society.

Existing rune stones tell a story of large, loving Viking families. One rune stone in Uppland, Sweden, carved in approximately the year 1000, reads, "Torsten caused this monument to be made in memory of Sven, his father, and of Tore, his brother, who were in Greece, and Ingletora, his mother."[8] Stones like this one—and there are many more—demonstrate the close, loving family structure the Vikings experienced, as well as just how far they traveled.

A CLASS SYSTEM

In many aspects, Viking society was tribal. Vikings lived in tight-knit groups that worked together to ensure the survival of everyone. In addition to *karls,* with whom much of Viking lore is associated, Viking society also included jarls and thralls.

The jarls, who were powerful, rich landowners, were essentially the heads of the tribes. As more people lived closer together and formed villages, the person with the most land—the jarl—often became the leader. Jarls were usually generous to their friends and followers. People went to the local jarl for guidance, as he also dispensed of justice locally. Sometimes jarls became so powerful and rich that they became kings in their own districts. Sometimes they fought one another in an effort to gain more territory, but it took many centuries before any one jarl became powerful enough to become a true king and rule the entire area.

The majority of people in Viking society were *karls. Karls* were freemen who also usually owned land, but not as much as a jarl. When a *karl* died, his land was passed down to his eldest son. Younger sons were left without land, but as freeborn men, they could earn enough money to buy land of their own either by working for other people or by looting and raiding. *Karls* were typically farmers, merchants, artisans, fishermen, craftsmen, and shipbuilders. The Viking merchants who established trading centers in other lands were also *karls.*

The third class of people in Viking society were thralls, or slaves. Thralls owned nothing and had no rights. If a thrall had children, they, too, were slaves.

VIKING KINGS

Many different groups, or tribes, existed during the Viking era. In the beginning, the power structure in Scandinavia was built on these tribes and the territories that they occupied. But as time went on, some tribes became more powerful and their territory grew more extensive.

In what was to become modern-day Sweden, two tribes emerged as the most influential: the Götar and the Svear. These tribes possessed large amounts of territory, or chiefdoms. Eventually these two chiefdoms became states, of sorts, and merged to become Sweden.

The two chiefdoms still exist today—in a manner of speaking. They are Götaland ("the Land of Götar") and Svealand ("the Land of Svear").

The traditional Viking societal unit was the tribe, led by a king.

WOMEN IN VIKING SOCIETY

A Viking woman's position in society was based on her father's or husband's standing. Even so, Viking women possessed many rights on their own. They ran the farms while the men were away raiding and trading. Women could conduct business on behalf of their husbands, shaking hands to seal the bargain—just like a man would do. The importance of women in society was shown by the fact that they possessed the household keys. Household keys secured the household and were also symbolic of control. A woman had the right to divorce her husband if he kept the household keys from her.

Even though most marriages were arranged by parents, many parents allowed their daughters to choose whether to go through with the match. Married women owned their own property and shared equally in any property the couple acquired during their marriage. If a woman was mistreated by her husband, she could divorce him. The woman would then take her property and return to her parents. In Viking society, men and women were free to divorce for any reason, and both parties were free to remarry after a divorce. Everything in Viking society was based on fairness—to the individual and particularly to the greater community.

A DEMOCRATIC SOCIETY

Sweden was one of the first areas in the world to develop a democratic form of government. The Vikings had great respect for the law and nearly all members of society participated in the democratic process. As far as researchers can tell, the Viking democratic process consisted of voting rights within the communal group.

Within each local community, an assembly called a *thing* controlled law and order. Each *thing* had its own set of laws and settled disputes between residents.

Most Vikings respected the laws and decisions handed down by the *things* because they preserved unity, harmony, and prosperity within the community. Any Viking who did not accept the decision of the *thing* became an outlaw and had to give up all of his or her land and possessions. Such outlaws usually also had to flee the community since they had no legal protection and could be killed by anyone—without punishment to the killer.

Viking raiding might seem like a direct contradiction to the concept of a democratic government and the preservation of the community. But while raiding certainly destroyed communities, it did not directly affect the Scandinavian communities. It was really outside of the legal arena. Throughout Viking society, the good of the whole community was of utmost importance.

THE END OF THE VIKING ERA

Just as the Vikings went forth raiding and colonizing new lands, they, too, were subject to colonization.

Unlike Christians, the Vikings believed in many gods, and as early as 829 missionaries from Europe set forth attempting to convert the Vikings to Christianity. In that year a French Benedictine monk named Ansgar (who later became Saint Ansgar) arrived in the trading town of Birka and began spreading the word of the gospel. Christianity was already taking hold throughout Europe, and as more and more missionaries arrived in Sweden, the belief in one Christian god gradually replaced the Vikings' original beliefs. Along with

Christianity came the tenet Love thy neighbor, and gradually the primary focus of Viking expeditions changed from raiding and acquiring new land to trading and its economic benefits.

With agricultural advancements at home and the development of larger trading centers, it was no longer necessary to raid and colonize new lands. Improved farming techniques made it possible to grow more and better crops. Advances in logging and clearing techniques also opened up more farmland.

In 1066 the last great Viking king, Harold III of Norway, was defeated by King Harold II of England. Harold II's own last name, Godwinson, was a Viking name. Only two days after Harold III's defeat, another Viking descendant, William of Normandy, invaded England. His troops crossed the English Channel in longships and conquered England. By 1100 the age of the Vikings was over.

Norse Gods

The Vikings worshiped a race of gods called the Aesir, and just like other early peoples, the Norsemen looked to these gods to explain natural events such as thunder, lightning, death, or love.

Thor was the mighty god of thunder. He carried a magical hammer named Mjölner, which created thunder when thrown; Mjölner then magically returned to him like a boomerang. Many Vikings carried charms shaped like Thor's hammer, which they felt would give them the god's protection. Thor even had his own day of the week: Thursday originally meant "Thor's Day."

Other gods were equally important. Odin was the god of war and wisdom. His warrior maidens, the Valkyries, chose the Viking warriors who would die heroically in battle and then led their spirits to Valhalla—a magical place where they could fight all day and feast all night. Other gods and goddesses represented phenomena like fertility and love.

With the rise of Christianity, pagan beliefs began to be replaced by the theory of one supreme god. Yet the tales of these adventuresome Norse gods still live today, thanks to the poems and sagas that were handed down through the generations and were finally written down during the 1200s. These sagas tell the stories of real Viking adventures as well as those of the gods.

Although Europeans hated and feared the Vikings during the years of their reign of terror, the end of the Viking age did not end their influence. Throughout the British Isles, Ireland, and the Baltic region, cities established by the Vikings are still flourishing. Many Vikings who settled in these foreign lands, such as King Harold II, assimilated into the local populace so effectively that they even managed to rise through the ranks and become kings.

Within Sweden, Viking influence still permeates many aspects of modern life. The Vikings' greatest legacies are a democratic government and a commitment to community welfare. In essence, the Vikings left a blueprint for modern Sweden's democratic government and ideology.

Kings and Wars

Following the Viking age, Sweden entered into a period of expansion and prosperity. Established towns gained further economic power, and within the region, the Swedes were beginning to develop a national identity. Christianity was widely accepted, although the influence of Viking traditions and concepts also remained strong.

But Sweden's Middle Ages was a turbulent time. Even as kings gained power within Sweden and throughout Scandinavia, they were elected by the people and limited by custom. The *things* still dealt with local problems, such as land ownership, theft, and divorce. This arrangement suited the people but made for an unstable monarchy initially. The presence of a council, and the threat of other nobles vying for the throne, meant that the king spent a lot of time seeking support from the aristocracy and trying to stay in their good graces. He might be the king of Sweden, but after all the political maneuvering, there was little time left over for him to actually accomplish much.

A Chief Among Equals

In 1280 King Magnus Ladulås became the first king of all of Sweden. Ladulås wanted a system in which the king was clearly at the top, taxes were paid to him, and he was essentially in charge of all land. This type of monarchy was called feudal, and it was the prevalent form of monarchies throughout Europe in the Middle Ages. Unfortunately for Ladulås, the whole idea went against the Viking concepts of freedom and fairness, and Swedish farmers banded together to block the implementation of a full feudal system.

The Swedes insisted on retaining their ancient rights and privileges—the original system of freeborn jarls and *karls*, landownership, and the legal authority of the *thing*. These ancient Viking rights had been handed down orally through successive generations, but in the face of an attempt to establish

King Magnus Ladulås tried to implement a feudal system in Sweden in which the king would hold ultimate control, but the plan went against Viking beliefs of individual freedom and was thus rejected.

a feudal form of government, the oral rights were written down and are now Europe's oldest body of written law.

While unity under a single leader did have advantages, namely stability in trade and foreign relations, Magnus Ladulås was never a king like his European counterparts. Elections and the presence of the *thing* curtailed his power. The Viking concepts of fairness and freedom were too deeply ingrained within the Swedes to permit one person to control everything.

SWEDEN AND THE HANSEATIC LEAGUE

For approximately the next two hundred years, starting with Ladulås, Sweden enjoyed a booming trade association with the European continent. Trade flourished between Sweden and Germany courtesy of the Hanseatic League, a trade association founded by German merchants. The Hanseatic League brought Sweden into peaceful contact with much of the European continent and exposed it to German influence. But while the Hanseatic League was a trade association, its influence extended far beyond simple commerce and trading. German influence overlapped into Sweden's political, social, and cultural areas as well. Even the Swedish language took on many of the linguistic forms spoken by the German traders.

Sweden's population eventually became concerned about Germany's growing influence on the country. While the Swedes enjoyed the benefits of trading through the Hanseatic League, they had no desire to become German.

THE UNION OF KALMAR

In 1397, in an effort to counterbalance the increasing influence of Germany and to consolidate the power of the monarchy, Sweden, Denmark, and the area now known as Norway formed the Union of Kalmar. The union was an agreement that Sweden, Denmark, and Norway would be united under the same monarchy. Although each country retained its own local government, all three would be subject to the Danish monarchy.

The Union of Kalmar lasted a little over one hundred years, until 1523, but it was a period that was marked by conflict rather than unity. The Swedish people never truly accepted the notion that Denmark was the dominant country of the union. Consequently, although Sweden was supposed to be in a union with Denmark, it was often at odds with the union's Danish monarchy. Ever since Magnus Ladulås, Sweden's sense of national identity had grown stronger, and the union was marked by a series of revolts by disgruntled Swedes.

In 1434 a Swede named Engelbrekt Engelbrektsson led a revolt against Erik of Pomerania, king of Denmark, Norway, and Sweden. King Erik was deposed, but the union continued. In 1471 another Swedish revolt was led by Sten Sture the

THE BLACK DEATH

Between 1347 and 1351, a great bubonic and pneumonic plague raged throughout Europe. Doctors could find no cure for those infected, and the disease raced uncontrollably across countries, killing millions.

The Black Death, as the plague of the 1300s was called, originated in Asia and reached Sweden by 1350. Within the next few years, approximately one-third of Sweden's entire population died.

Losing this much of its population had a severe effect on the Swedish economy, as there were fewer people available to work and many farms were abandoned after the owners died. It took more than one hundred years for Sweden to fully recover from the effects of the Black Death.

Elder. At the ensuing Battle of Brunkeberg, the Swedes won decisively, yet the union managed to endure for another fifty years.

THE BLOODBATH OF STOCKHOLM

In an attempt to rid himself of Swedish troublemakers, King Christian II of Denmark and Norway ordered the execution of eighty-two Swedish citizens in 1520. The Bloodbath of Stockholm, as it came to be called, incited a rebellion that led to Christian's downfall and, effectively, ended the Union of Kalmar.

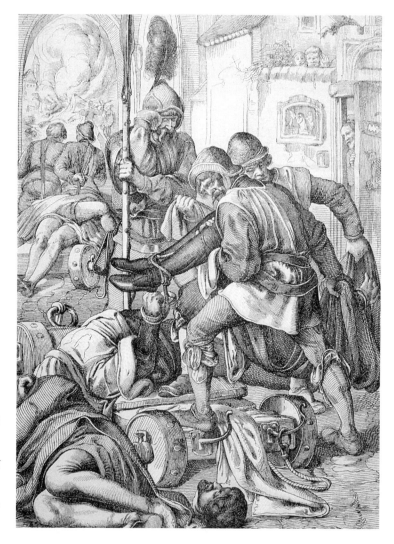

The bodies of massacred Swedish nobles who opposed the rule of the Danish king Christian II are carried to the city gates to be burned during the Bloodbath of Stockholm.

The leader of the rebellion was Swedish nobleman Gustav Eriksson Vasa, whose father and relatives had been murdered in the Bloodbath of Stockholm. Vasa proved to be a competent and determined leader, and under his direction, Sweden dissolved the Union of Kalmar. In 1523, by consensus of the other "rebels," or noblemen, Vasa was crowned king of Sweden. The reforms he proceeded to initiate can still be observed in Sweden's present-day government.

THE VASA DYNASTY

Vasa was the patriarch of a dynasty that would rule Sweden for approximately the next two hundred years. Known as the Great Power Period, it was marked by prosperity, expansion, and war.

One of Vasa's first acts as king was to take over the property of the Roman Catholic Church within Sweden and turn the church into a national institution—with the full approval of the parliament.

In founding the Church of Sweden, Vasa took control of the monasteries, most of them brimming with riches. Although the Catholic Church made several peaceful attempts to regain its property and power in Sweden, with each successive king the Church of Sweden, or Lutheran Church, became stronger. By the mid-1600s Sweden was entirely Protestant Lutheran.

Creating a state-controlled church accomplished several things. The king, not the pope, became the head of the church. By controlling the pulpit, the king could put forth his views and ideology every Sunday—to a captive audience. It was a useful way for the king to reinforce his leadership and effectively set Sweden apart from the other Scandinavian and European countries in which the church and the state were still relatively separate institutions that were often at odds with each other.

A HEREDITARY MONARCHY

In addition to taking control of the church, Gustav Vasa both declared the monarchy hereditary in 1544 and streamlined government administrative positions, modeling them after more efficient methods. Both of these changes—a more efficient government and a hereditary monarchy—gave the king the tools and time to effectively run the country.

Vasa is also credited with establishing a monarchy based on democratic principles and the Viking ideal of a king being a leader among equals. According to Navigo, a Swedish

THE CHURCH OF SWEDEN TODAY

The Church of Sweden is still the dominant faith of the Swedish people, claiming more than 90 percent of the population as members. But church membership rates are high because Swedish children automatically become members of the Church of Sweden at birth if one of their parents is a member. Sweden is basically a secular, or nonreligious, state, and only about 5 percent of the population attend church on a regular basis.

Even though Sweden has an official national church, there is religious freedom within the country. Since 1781, when the Edict of Toleration was issued, other religions have been accepted and tolerated in Sweden. In 1952 full religious freedom was guaranteed by law. Swedish parents can also renounce membership on behalf of their child within six weeks after birth. Other members may apply to leave the church at any time.

While few Swedes attend church on a regular basis, nearly all Swedes observe the Christian customs of marrying in the church, baptizing and confirming their children in the church, and having burial services performed by the church.

Although the church's influence on the Swedish people does not appear to be very strong, a strong bond between the church, the state, and the parliament still exists. From the 1600s until 1991, the Church of Sweden maintained all of the national population records.

website, "He personally wrote letters even to common farmers, telling them how to do things and solve problems."[9] Even though Vasa embodied democratic principles and Viking ideology, he was still the king and, as such, could exert his will and influence rapidly and with little recourse. Navigo goes on to say,

> Some hundred years later in history when a quite romanticized picture of the king was drawn, this was used as an example of his greatness and one of the facts that, for many generations of Swedes, made him a beloved monarch. The people who received critical letters from King Gustav Vasa probably did not think of him as a "beloved monarch." Most people were presumably terrified.[10]

Although Vasa concentrated much power into his own hands, or in the office of king, history still remembers him as a fair and just ruler.

The Years of Power

During Sweden's Great Power Period, there was a great deal of turmoil in the surrounding countries. The breakup of the German government disrupted established trade routes. In response, England established a new trade route north of Sweden going into Russia—effectively bypassing Sweden. As a nation whose livelihood was tied to trading, Sweden was displeased and tried to aggressively take control of all of the northern regions of Scandinavia, which, in turn, led to conflicts with Russia and Denmark. Additionally at this time Russia was involved in a civil war. In an attempt to take advantage of the chaotic situation, Sweden took part in this war. As a result, when a Russian peace treaty was finally signed, Sweden ended up controlling Finland.

In 1630 Gustavus II Adolph, a descendant of Gustav Vasa, entered into the Thirty Years' War that was raging across Europe.

Swedish king Gustavus II Adolph receives a fatal shot at the 1632 Battle of Lützen during the Thirty Years' War.

With the breakup of the Hanseatic League at least fifty years prior, Germany's powerful, organized government had ceased to exist. In the interim, Sweden had established its own trade routes. But Germany's strength was again growing, and Sweden feared that a powerful Germany was a threat to its own trading in the Baltic region.

Although all of the countries around it were in chaos, within its own boundaries, Sweden was enjoying a period of great prosperity. Under the leadership of strong dynasties and an efficient Riksdag, Sweden's economy was strong and well managed. Its domestic iron and weapons industries were booming as Sweden kept the surrounding warring region supplied with arms. Within the boundaries of Sweden, the populace was prosperous and flourishing.

All of these factors—a strong economy, booming industry, and chaos among its neighbors—worked to Sweden's advantage. But according to Navigo's website,

> The external factors, a weak Russia and social and economic problems in other European countries that competed with Sweden, are regarded by most scholars as the main explanation as to why Sweden, with its limited resources, could become so powerful.[11]

Still, even if Sweden was prosperous, being constantly at war was expensive. Only a small portion of Sweden's troops in Europe were Swedes or Finns; the rest were mercenaries, or paid foreign soldiers. Even with a strong economy, paying for these soldiers was devastating the state finances. When Gustavus II died, he left the next king with a military and economic mess.

THE END OF THE GREAT POWER PERIOD

By the mid-1600s Sweden encompassed vast amounts of territory. Present-day Finland, Estonia, Latvia, and regions of Germany were all part of Sweden, and the defense of these extended borders was becoming difficult and costly.

In 1697 King Karl XI died. He had ruled Sweden with a firm hand and was responsible for much of Sweden's expansion and rise to power. His fifteen-year-old son, Karl XII, succeeded him on the throne. King Karl XI had claimed new territories, but with a young and inexperienced king on the Swedish throne, Russia, Norway, Denmark, and Poland saw their chance to regain their lost territories. They formed an alliance and attacked, thus starting the Great Nordic War in 1700.

Although the war initially went well for Sweden, by 1709 the Swedish army was almost annihilated. Russia had conquered the Baltic provinces as well as the greater part of Finland, and some of Sweden's territories in northern Germany had also been lost.

In 1718 King Karl XII was killed during a battle in southern Norway. In a peace treaty signed in 1721, Sweden lost all of its Baltic provinces, most of Finland, and nearly all of its territories in northern Germany. By 1721 Sweden's frontiers were reduced to roughly the borders of present-day Sweden and Finland.

The Vasa Legacy

The Vasa dynasty continued for another ninety years. It finally came to an inglorious end in 1808, when the last of Gustav Vasa's descendants was dethroned after losing the Finnish territory. But the Vasa legacy remains. The hereditary monarchy is still in place, and constitutional reforms instituted during the Vasa dynasty remained in place until 1974. Although Sweden's Great Power Period effectively ended with the death of Karl XII, Sweden was still left with a strong parliamentarian government and a booming economy.

Thanks to the Vasa dynasty, Sweden still has a rich artistic and cultural tradition as well as a national religion. With Gustav III's ascension to the throne in 1771, even Swedish culture made enormous advances. Gustav III founded the Swedish Academy for Literature, Music, Art, and History and Antiques. He was also responsible for building the Royal Opera House and establishing the Royal Dramatic Theater in Stockholm.

War and Changing Borders

Gustav III was the last of the strong Vasa kings. As his influence increased, so did the discontent of the Swedish aristocracy. Upset over their own loss of power, the aristocrats plotted to have Gustav III assassinated, and in 1792 he was murdered during a masked opera ball. After the death of Gustav III, his son Gustav IV Adolph succeeded him. He was not as strong a ruler as his father. In 1808 Sweden went to war against Russia and ended up losing Finland. After this fiasco,

THE *VASA*

When Gustavus II Adolph was preparing to take Sweden into the Thirty Years' War, he commissioned a sumptuous warship, the *Vasa*. Built in the 1620s, the *Vasa* was one of the most elaborate warships of the time.

In 1628 the ship was finished and ready for launching. Loaded with men and weapons, it majestically cast off from the dock and sailed into present-day Stockholm's harbor. Its maiden voyage ended, though, almost before it began. Apparently, a sudden gust of wind caught its sails, capsizing the *Vasa* and sending it to the bottom of the harbor. For more than three centuries, the ship lay on the harbor bottom covered with mud.

In 1956 the *Vasa* was rediscovered, and in 1961 a salvage operation managed to raise the ship to the surface. The hull was intact, and the ship was almost perfectly preserved since the low salt content of the Baltic's water cannot support the worms that usually eat through ship timbers.

Today the *Vasa* is housed in its own museum in Stockholm. More than twenty-four thousand items have been recovered from the ship's harbor location, and marine archaeologists have been putting the warship back together like a giant jigsaw puzzle.

The magnificent warship Vasa, *salvaged from the bottom of the Stockholm harbor, now rests in a museum.*

In 1810 Sweden elected French field marshal Jean-Baptiste-Jules Bernadotte to become King Charles XIV John.

a disgruntled Riksdag dethroned Gustav IV and enacted sweeping constitutional changes that limited the power of the monarchy even further by dividing power between the king, the parliament, and the courts. This constitution was so effective that it endured without any change until 1974.

The loss of Finland also produced an association with France that endures, indirectly, even today. With the dethroning of Gustav IV Adolph, succession to the Swedish throne was uncertain. There were no more Vasas to succeed to the Swedish throne, and among Sweden's own aristocracy, the choices were disheartening when it came to choosing someone strong enough to lead the country. At the same time, Napoléon was a strong French general and leader. As a solution to its problem, the Swedish parliament elected one of Napoléon's field marshals to be the new king of Sweden. Jean-Baptiste-Jules Bernadotte, who became known as King Charles XIV John, succeeded to the Swedish throne in 1810, although he was not actually sworn in until 1818. Ever since, all of Sweden's monarchs have been descended from Bernadotte—including Sweden's current monarch.

Sweden ended the eighteenth century with strong social, economic, and governmental structures already taking shape. With smaller borders to defend and no war to occupy all of its time, Sweden was poised to develop its own unique form of modern government, social services for its citizens, and a military presence devoted to peace.

DEVELOPING A MODERN NATION

4

From birth to death, Sweden's government pervades nearly every aspect of modern Swedish life. From health care to education, guaranteed employment, free cultural events, and even burial rites in the Church of Sweden—the Swedish government is ever present in the lives of its populace.

Swedes believe that every citizen is entitled to a minimum standard of living, and to that end, they have developed a governmental system that assures that everyone receives an education, job training, decent housing, and necessary medical care. To implement this fair standard of living for all, the government controls and administers these areas for the common good of the Swedish population.

The Swedish government also provides retirement pensions and child care. Likewise, if Swedes cannot work due to illness, injury, or unemployment, the government provides them with allowances to help maintain their homes and families.

At the head of the government is the king, but as a constitutional monarchy, the Swedish throne is only ceremonial. The real power of the Swedish government lies with the Riksdag—the parliament. The Riksdag, whose members are elected entirely by the people, controls nearly all legal, political, and social aspects of Swedish life, just as its predecessor, the *thing*, did.

THE CONSTITUTIONAL MONARCHY TODAY

Since 1973 Carl XVI Gustaf has been the king of Sweden. He and his wife, the German-born Queen Silvia, have three children. In 1980 the four-hundred-year-old order of succession was changed so that the eldest child now inherits the throne regardless of gender. Consequently, Princess Victoria, who was born in 1977, will become the queen of Sweden upon her father's death.

45

Sweden's royal family, who has resided outside Stockholm in Drottningholm Palace since 1982, is quite beloved by the Swedish people. Although only a ceremonial position, the present king is involved in many environmental matters, and most Swedes feel that he is an excellent representative of the country.

Although the idea of abolishing the monarchy entirely has occasionally come up within the Riksdag, most representatives, along with the people of Sweden, are content with the role the monarchy plays in modern Swedish life. Unlike the monarchy of Great Britain, for instance, the Swedish monarchy costs the Swedish taxpayers very little to maintain.

 ## POLITICAL PARTIES AND THE MIDDLE WAY

For more than a century, Sweden's "middle way" worked very well, allowing the Swedish people to enjoy a high standard of living—courtesy of high taxes and the welfare state—while their economy prospered under private ownership. The political party most responsible for this system is the Social Democrats. Since the late 1920s, it has been the political party most continuously in control of the Riksdag and is credited with the development of Sweden's welfare state. But Sweden has several political parties.

Until the 1988 elections, five political parties dominated Swedish politics: the Social Democrats, the Conservatives, the Liberals, the Center Party, and the Left Wing. By the end of the 1980s, environmental issues had come to the forefront, and a new party emerged in the 1988 elections. The Green Party received 5.5 percent of the votes cast during that election and, consequently, received twenty seats in the Riksdag.

Although Sweden has more than two political parties, its form of government is still referred to as a modified two-party system primarily because all of the parties tend to divide along one of two lines: liberal or conservative. Most of Sweden's political parties formed due to popular movements, such as the labor, temperance, or nonconformist movements, at the turn of the last century. With such origins, each party has been strong within different segments of Swedish society.

King Carl XVI Gustav and Queen Silvia hold a ceremonial, rather than authoritative, position under Sweden's constitutional monarchy.

The Modern-Day Riksdag

The first line of the Swedish constitution states that "All public power in Sweden comes from the people," so even though the king is Sweden's head of state, he exercises no power or authority in governing the state. It is the government, the Regering (which consists of the prime minister and his cabinet), that governs the state and is answerable to the Riksdag (the parliament).

The house of parliament in Stockholm, where the Riksdag meets. The unicameral Riksdag elects the prime minister and votes on bills.

Sweden's Riksdag is a unicameral, or one-house, system composed of 349 members. Each member of the Riksdag is elected for a four-year term.

Any Swede eighteen years or older has the right to vote. Any non-Swede who has been living in Sweden for at least three years has the right to vote in local, but not national, elections. The percentage of people who vote during elections is one of the highest in the world; approximately 90 percent of the Swedish population votes in every election.

The Prime Minister

Unlike in many countries, the prime minister of Sweden is not directly elected by the people. Instead, Sweden's prime minister is nominated and elected by the Riksdag. After a general election, the chairman of the Riksdag proposes a candidate to be the new prime minister. The proposed candidate is usually the head of the political party that won the most votes in the election. All members of the Riksdag then vote for or against the candidate. The new prime minister then selects the rest of his cabinet and appoints many of the ministers. The prime minister also has the right to dismiss the ministers.

PRIME MINISTER OLOF PALME

Olof Palme held the position of prime minister of Sweden from 1982 to 1986. On February 28, 1986, Palme and his wife were walking home after seeing a movie when a gunman shot and killed him.

The assassination stunned Sweden and the world. Sweden has a well-deserved reputation as a peaceful, safe country. In 1990, for instance, Sweden had only 121 deaths from murder, manslaughter, or assaults—an exceedingly low number. Because the Riksdag, or the people, maintain the true power, Swedes had never considered the job of prime minister to be particularly risky. Olof Palme did not live his life surrounded by an entourage of secret service police; he lived and worked like most other Swedes—witness the fact that he and his wife were walking home alone after the movie, not being whisked into an armored limousine after a private showing.

After the assassination, many Swedes were angry and disillusioned. The crime has never been completely solved and continues to trouble the nation. Despite its anger over the assassination, Sweden remains an outspoken proponent for world peace and a nonviolent lifestyle.

The assassination of Prime Minister Olof Palme remains unsolved.

Within the government there are thirteen ministries. These relatively small agencies are primarily concerned with the preparation of new government bills, which will then be approved or rejected by the Riksdag. All laws are enforced by approximately one hundred independent central administrative agencies and twenty-four local county administrative agencies.

LOCAL CONTACT WITH THE GOVERNMENT

In the rich tradition of the *thing*, the Swedish government has maintained a policy of giving its people a great deal of local control in government matters. Sweden currently has 288 local municipalities throughout the country. These locally elected councils collect the local income tax and administer public services such as the schools, utilities, housing, child and elder care services, and cultural and leisure activities. The local councils are also responsible for operating the health care systems in their areas.

THE OMBUDSMAN

Sweden's government has a special department whose only purpose is to protect the individual rights of the Swedish people in their contact with actual government authorities. The officials of this department are called ombudsmen, and they are appointed to four-year terms by the Riksdag.

Ombudsmen (who can also be women) listen to complaints from Swedish citizens about the actions or decisions of other government agencies. The ombudsmen act like judges if a government agency acts in a manner that displeases any private citizen. They have the power to investigate any situation. They listen to both sides, decide which side is correct, and take disciplinary action against the offending agency, if they feel it is necessary. Areas of special interest to ombudsmen are the rights of children, ethnic discrimination, equal opportunity, newspapers, and consumer affairs.

THE MIDDLE WAY

When it comes to the health and general welfare of its people, Sweden has found that socialized programs work well. But when it comes to industry and the economy, Sweden's government has adopted a hands-off policy. When a government does not interfere with or control private industry, the government is referred to as a capitalist government. Combining both socialism and capitalism is difficult to do, but Sweden has managed quite nicely. Sweden's philosophy is often described as "the middle way"—meaning it has struck a working balance between socialism and capitalism. It also means that Sweden likes to take a careful and moderate stance on most issues, both local and international.

How this tiny nation has managed to combine socialism, to produce a uniformly high standard of living for its people, with capitalism, to produce a strong economy, is baffling to many observers in the international community. For within the global community, Sweden is an economically strong country, and its people do enjoy one of the highest standards of living on the planet. Other nations that have tried to function on a purely socialist or purely capitalist basis have not done nearly so well—and virtually no nation has been able to combine the two as seamlessly as Sweden has.

More than 85 percent of Swedish industry is privately owned. Sweden's policy of having its industry be privately owned seems to have worked, for Sweden is one of the wealthiest and most technologically advanced countries in the world. But its periods of prosperity have been interwoven with periods of great hardship.

FROM POVERTY TO BOOMING INDUSTRY

Although Swedes have a history of being shrewd businessmen dating back to the Viking age, Sweden was not always the wealthy and technologically advanced nation it is today. As recently as the 1800s, Sweden was a poor farming nation. Work was hard to find in Sweden, and there was not enough farmland available to grow food and make a living. Around 1860 the economy was in such bad shape that hundreds of thousands of Swedes immigrated to the United States.

Sweden's rise as an industrial nation got its biggest boost from the development of hydroelectric power. With an abundance of rivers and waterfalls in the northern part of the country, Sweden figured out how to produce electricity through hydropower. This provided the country with a cheap, clean source of power and substantially lowered the costs of industrial production. Today, more than half of Sweden's electricity still comes from hydropower. The rest comes primarily from twelve nuclear reactor plants and a few oil-burning plants.

Sweden has an abundance of natural, raw materials such as lumber and iron ore. Sweden used its natural resources to fuel its own development, but the country also exported a great deal. Within the last century, Sweden's forestry industry became even more export oriented. Sweden's sawmill industry is still the largest in Europe, accounting for 10 percent of all sawmill products that are exported worldwide.

The Volvo assembly line. Volvo automobiles are one of the most well known Swedish exports.

Modern Sweden has retained the Viking practice of exporting goods around the globe. Sweden is one of the top ten iron exporters in the world. In the mining sector alone, for example, 90 percent of all production is exported, and in the early 1990s Sweden was the third-largest exporter of pulp and paper products in the world. Today, Sweden's steel industry remains strong because it concentrates on quality and specialization. More than half of Sweden's steel-export income comes from the sale of specialized steel used in precision tools and instruments.

THE COST OF "THE MIDDLE WAY"

Sweden's prosperity, both social and economic, comes at a price. To be able to fund the services the government provides, Swedes pay some of the highest taxes in the world. Every Swede pays approximately 30 percent of his or her income to the government in taxes. It is these taxes that pay for Sweden's high standard of living. Everyone must contribute so that the community as a whole will be prosperous. A commitment to peace is part of that prosperity.

Swedish Inventions

Despite its small population, Sweden is the home country of a large number of inventions.

Dynamite. During an experiment, the Swedish chemist Alfred Nobel accidentally broke a bottle of nitroglycerin. The chemical mixed with the material protecting the bottle, creating a product with the same explosive effect as pure nitroglycerin but much less dangerous to handle. Nobel called his invention dynamite. Dynamite earned Nobel so much money that he was able to create the Nobel Foundation, which annually awards the coveted Nobel Prizes.

Zipper. Although the first patent for a zipper was obtained by an American, the zipper was invented by two Swedes: Peter Aronsson and Gideon Sundback. Since 1913, their zipper has been the manufacturing model for zippers the world over.

Propeller. In 1836 John Ericsson of Sweden patented the device that is now commonly used for ships and aircraft. The propeller is only one of many things invented, or improved on, by Ericsson. In the United States, he is also known for constructing the battleship *Monitor,* which was used by the North during the American Civil War.

Safety Match. Matches are not a Swedish invention, but the obsolete ones often set fire to their users as well as to candles and cigars. In 1844 Gustaf Erik Pasch improved the match, creating the modern-day safety match.

Modern Telephone. Original telephones had a mouthpiece built into them, while the speaker was connected to the phone through flex cording. In 1876 Lars Magnus Ericsson had the idea to combine the two into a single receiver, creating the telephone as we know it today. He founded the Ericsson Company, which is still a powerful communications company that exports the world over.

Tetra Pak. In 1944 Swedes Erik Wallenberg and Ruben Rausing invented a paper packaging system for noncarbonated liquids. Particularly useful for dairy products, their invention is commonly called a milk carton.

In stark contrast to its violent Viking past, since the early 1800s Sweden has been a peaceful country. For nearly two hundred years, the Swedish government has focused its efforts on economic growth and a prosperous lifestyle for its inhabitants. Jean-Baptiste-Jules Bernadotte's war against

Napoléon, fought in the early 1800s, was the last war in which Sweden participated. Today, Sweden maintains a policy of strict neutrality, insisting on nonalignment during peacetime and nonparticipation during war—although the nation has always registered an opinion on international matters.

Sweden's evolution from violence to neutrality may seem baffling. But above all else, Swedes are devoted to fairness, personal freedoms, and what is best for all concerned. If a nation is always at war, it is more difficult to develop a prosperous economy and a decent lifestyle for its people.

Swedish sailors visit at a naval base. Military service in either the navy, army, or air force is compulsory for men age twenty to forty-seven.

Neutrality also does not mean that Sweden remains isolated. Sweden has been very active in the United Nations since its founding in 1955, and Swedish soldiers take part in UN peacekeeping operations. Swedish UN soldiers have been part of UN peacekeeping forces in Somalia, Bosnia, the Congo, Cyprus, and the Middle East.

Sweden also maintains an active foreign policy although, in keeping with its policy of neutrality, Sweden has never been, and does not plan to become, a member of the North Atlantic Treaty Organization (NATO). NATO is an organization of countries in the region of the North Atlantic Ocean. Its membership includes the United States and many European countries. NATO is devoted to keeping peace within the region, even if it means using military force—which is why Sweden refuses to join.

In order to preserve its neutrality, Sweden must maintain a large defense force that is always ready to defend its borders and maintain its status as a neutral nation as well as contribute toward international peacekeeping efforts. Since 1901 Sweden has had a policy of compulsory military service, meaning that every man between the ages of eighteen and forty-seven is legally required to serve in the Swedish military. At age eighteen, all men are called to a conscription to determine if they are fit for military service. At that point it is decided which branch of the military they will be in: army, air force, or navy. At age twenty, Swedish men are actually drafted and spend between seven and fifteen months doing basic training. From then on, until the age of forty-seven, Swedish men are regularly called back for military refresher courses. This compulsory service is an obligation and commitment to Sweden's policy of "the middle way," along with their membership in the United Nations.

Sweden is likewise committed to its education system and job training programs, and the nation's workforce is highly skilled. Sweden has a reputation for producing quality products such as technologically advanced communication equipment, crystal products, woven textiles, and sleekly designed wooden furniture. Even with funding educational job training and worker benefits, Sweden has typically been able to produce quality export products cheaper than other nations.

But Sweden's commitment remains to its people, not the actual products they produce. This, too, creates additional tax burdens on the populace. Because of socialized government programs, every worker is able to live decently, no matter what their occupation or actual earnings. Whatever job a person holds, thanks to government subsidies, there is very little distinction between Swedes' lifestyles.

5

THE FACE OF SWEDEN TODAY

Sweden has nearly 9 million people, the largest population of any Scandinavian country. Even so, Sweden is one of the least-densely populated nations in Europe, with more than half of the country claiming fewer than twenty-five people per square mile (ten per square kilometer). The majority of Sweden's population is concentrated in metropolitan areas, leaving vast tracts of natural landscape throughout the country. Four out of five Swedes live in urban areas, with nearly one-third of the population living in Stockholm, Göteborg, or Malmö. Most of these urban dwellers live in apartment buildings.

Much of Sweden's population is homogeneous, or very similar in appearance. Because of Sweden's geographical isolation from the rest of Europe, few people, other than the ancient original Germanic tribes, migrated to Scandinavia. Consequently, the genetic makeup of most Swedes has changed very little over the centuries. Even today, although it is not unusual to see Swedes with brown hair and brown eyes, much of the population has blond hair and blue eyes— a testimony to their Germanic ancestors.

In the 1940s Sweden experienced a postwar influx of immigrants because of the nation's policy of neutrality, which enabled it to emerge from World War II relatively unscathed. The industrial and economic structures of other nations were devastated by the war, but Sweden's were intact and in need of workers. As a result, many foreign laborers immigrated to Sweden to help meet the demand for Swedish products in the postwar world. Although the influx of immigrants created a more diversified population, Sweden still remains very homogeneous. Finns are the largest minority group, and only about 13 percent of Sweden's population either was born in another country or has one parent who was born elsewhere.

MARRIAGE AND SWEDISH FAMILIES

Families have remained an important part of Swedish life since Viking times. However, marriage is not always a part of family life. Cohabitation, or living together, is common in Sweden. In 1987 nearly half of all children born in Sweden were born to parents who were not married.

The Swedish language even has a special word for people who live together without being married. *Sambo* refers to the person someone is living with, either male or female. *Sambos* are treated exactly like husbands or wives—except that they are not legally married to their partners.

A couple's marital status does not affect the social or legal standing of their children. There is no social stigma attached to children of unmarried parents, nor does the Swedish government make any distinctions between the children of married and unmarried couples. Some couples decide to marry after several years of living together—and their children attend the wedding. Other children spend their whole lives

Many Swedes today, like their Germanic ancestors, have blond hair and blue eyes.

A young family strolls through a narrow Stockholm street flanked by buildings. Most Swedish people live in apartment buildings in such urban areas.

with parents who never marry. Still others have parents who separate, and their time is divided between both parents—just like a child whose parents are divorced.

Marriage has not gone out of style; people still get married in Sweden. But with about half of all marriages ending in divorce, Sweden has one of the highest divorce rates in the Western world, comparable to that of the United States. Although divorces are relatively easy to obtain, the Swedish government requires that all couples applying for divorce go through mandatory counseling. Still, sociologists are uncertain why Sweden's divorce statistics are so high.

WORKING FAMILIES

Sweden is an expensive place to live. Although many people own small summer cottages, the majority of the population lives in apartment buildings in the larger urban areas such as Stockholm. Houses are very expensive, and even the rent on an apartment can be costly. The high cost of living, on top of the high taxes Swedes pay, means that few families can live the way they want to on just one income. Usually both partners work.

Sweden has a long history of treating women equally, from Viking marriage laws to thirteenth-century laws guaranteeing equality and protection to Sweden's present-day government. Today, Swedish women have achieved more equality in the workforce than women from most other nations; 82 percent of all Swedish women, mothers and nonmothers, work.

SWEDISH CHILDREN

Children are highly regarded in Swedish society, and the government has taken great pains to ensure that all children receive proper care. When a baby is born, the state provides an allowance for one parent to stay home with the child for one year, while still receiving 90 percent of his or her work salary. An additional ninety days can also be taken, with slightly reduced pay.

In addition to a liberal maternity leave policy, the government also ensures that children are treated with respect. There is a special ombudsman to deal with the rights of children, and it is against the law to hit a child. Anyone who does so faces going to jail. Other countries, including the United States, have laws against child abuse, but a love and respect for children has been so deeply ingrained in the Swedish culture that child abuse is extremely rare. The ombudsman agency concerned with children's rights is extremely diligent about enforcing the law in what few cases of child abuse there are.

With both parents typically working, the state also provides many social services for families. In addition to high-quality free education, the government also provides day care and will work individually with parents who might need additional help with their children, such as those parents whose children may be handicapped or have other special needs. Even with both parents working, children and adults spend a lot of time together sharing activities.

EDUCATION FOR ALL

Since 1842 education has been compulsory in Sweden—that is, every child between the ages of seven and sixteen must attend school. All schooling in Sweden is free, including the books, supplies, and hot lunches. Free transportation and clothing are also available to children who need them, as is free schooling for children with hearing, vision, or speech impairments and for the mentally handicapped.

Until the 1980s, the Swedish curriculum did not take into account Sami culture, language, or lifestyle. Because of the country's educational policies, the rich heritage of the Sami was in danger of dying out. Nowadays, Swedish schools located in Sami regions (the Lapland portions of Norrland) incorporate Sami heritage into the curriculum.

SAMI: THE "OTHER" SWEDES

Sweden's aboriginal people, the Sami, were originally nomads. They herded reindeer, lived in tents, and followed the reindeer as they migrated. Today, reindeer still feature prominently in Sami culture and lifestyle, but herding methods have been modernized. Most Sami live in settlements and use modern equipment, such as snowmobiles, to keep track of their herds. The Sami also perform a variety of occupations besides reindeer herding. In fact, most Sami live no differently than their Scandinavian neighbors.

The Sami have their own language, which is related to the Finnish, Hungarian, and Estonian languages. But because the Sami have led a nomadic existence throughout the Arctic Circle region, as many as nine languages have evolved.

In the 1950s the Sami of Norway, Sweden, and Finland formed an association to deal with the challenge of keeping their culture and lifestyle alive. Nowadays, the Nordic Sami Council oversees the affairs of Lapland. In 1973 the council founded the Nordic Sami Institute. Located in Norway and set right in the heart of reindeer country, the institute promotes the study of the Sami language and culture.

In the last few decades, the Scandinavian governments have accorded more recognition and power to the Sami. The Sami of Finland have had their own parliament since 1976, and in 1980 and 1982 Norway and Sweden, respectively, established Sami Rights Commissions. The commissions recommended that both countries set up separate Sami parliaments.

Foreign language study is a mandatory part of the curriculum, beginning in third grade with English instruction. In seventh grade, children choose an additional language they would like to learn, such as German or Italian.

In eighth grade, Swedish children get a chance to find out about future occupations that might interest them. They spend time as aides in schools, hospitals, mechanical shops, and other places. By ninth grade, students must choose a course of study in one of three areas: arts and social studies, science and technical studies, or economic and commercial studies. Students who plan on pursuing a university education go to schools called gymnasiums for the U.S. equivalent of tenth, eleventh, and twelfth grades. In Sweden, though,

With the establishment of parliaments and cooperative educational systems, the Sami are attempting to preserve their lifestyle and a healthy economy for the residents of Lapland. The 1986 Chernobyl nuclear meltdown in the Ukraine had a disastrous effect on Lapland. The reindeer herds became contaminated with radioactive fallout, and the meat could not be sold. The herders were not adequately compensated, and as a result, the Sami economy was devastated.

Such global incidents have made the Sami realize that they cannot remain isolated from the rest of the world. In Sweden they may be the Sami, but they are also Swedes. As such, they are demanding a more active role in their destiny and in the affairs of Sweden.

A Sami in traditional formal wear. The Sami live in Lapland across northern Scandinavia.

students choose tracks of study that vary in length of time required.

COMPETITIVE HIGHER EDUCATION

Until 1993 all higher education was under one government system. But a new Higher Education Act in 1993 offered more autonomy and diversity to separate universities, while still retaining most of the original system.

According to the website Navigo,

The purpose of the institutions of higher education, as stated in the Higher Education Act of 1993, is to provide education and carry out research and artistic development; there should be a close connection between these two main duties. Emphasis is placed on quality and the effective use of available resources. Equality between men and women should be observed in all aspects of higher education. Universities and university colleges should also promote an understanding of other countries and international relationships.[12]

About one-third of all gymnasium graduates go on to universities. University tuition is free, and in some cases, the state even pays for the student's living expenses. One reason for the small number of gymnasium graduates attending universities is that a limited number of spaces are available. Since 1991, though, the government has steadily expanded the number of places for university undergraduate studies, adding more professors and classes, and by the mid-1990s most Swedish universities had increased their acceptance of students by about 30 percent. But getting into a Swedish university is still very competitive, and not all students who want to study at a university are accepted. Fortunately, universities are not the only option for continuing education.

Scandinavia has a tradition of "folk schools." Folk schools are a type of boarding school in which adults can take courses lasting from twenty to thirty-four weeks, usually during the

SMORGASBORD!

Every nation has food products that are unique to its country. But Sweden developed a particular way of eating—the smorgasbord, or buffet meal—that has become renowned around the world. The word *smorgasbord* has come to mean a spectacular feast with lots of items to choose from, but the word really means "open sandwich table." The smorgasbord is a Swedish tradition and can be found in homes and restaurants throughout the year, but Christmastime is when they are most abundant.

As Christmas draws nearer, many families spend much time preparing a lavish smorgasbord. A smorgasbord nearly always contains several herring dishes (including sweet-pickled herring or pickled herring with onions, mustard, and dill), meatballs, salmon, salads, and "Jansson's temptation" (sliced herring, potatoes, and onions baked in cream). Always present are eggs, bread, boiled and fried potatoes, and, of course, numerous sweets or desserts at the end.

winter. In addition to taking courses in handicrafts and other hobbies, adults who did not finish high school can make up the missed courses at a folk school. Many companies in Sweden also offer special training courses for their employees to help them acquire skills that are useful on the job.

Nearly one-third of all adults in Sweden take part in some form of adult education. In the evenings, regular school buildings are used for adult classes. Other school facilities, such as swimming pools and gyms, are also open after hours for public use.

AN ACTIVE LIFESTYLE

When not working or in school, Swedes love to be outdoors—even their celebrations revolve around the outdoors. Sweden is a nation of athletes, and more than half of the population belongs to at least one community sports association or company sports club. The nation has participated in the Olympic Games since the first modern games started in 1896. Since that time, Sweden has won more than five hundred Olympic medals, including more than two hundred gold medals.

Sweden's oldest sport is skiing, although for many years it was not thought of as a sport—it was a means of transportation. Ancient skis were nearly nine feet long and six inches wide. As early as 1200, Swedish ski troops were used in battle. Recreational skiing, as we know it today, is only about two hundred years old. There are downhill slopes and ski jumps throughout Sweden, and thousands of Swedes participate in cross-country ski races each winter. The annual Vasa Race is held on the first Sunday in March and commemorates King Gustav Vasa's escape from the Bloodbath of Stockholm. More than twelve thousand cross-country skiers participate each year.

In Sweden, sports are considered an important part of a healthy lifestyle. Swedes take the motto Sport for all very seriously. Children and physically handicapped people participate in sports on a regular basis. Girls are encouraged to participate in sports as much as boys. Families hike and camp together, using the hundreds of miles of trails that exist in the mountains and forests. Every summer the O-ringen, a five-day orienteering race, attracts more than twenty thousand people—all of whom run cross-country and use a compass and map for direction.

RECREATION IN THE ARCHIPELAGO

For many residents of Stockholm, the city is where they live and work, but the islands are where they play. Stockholm's archipelago of islands stretches nearly ninety miles along the coastline and provides countless opportunities for recreation. As author Charles N. Barnard points out in the July/August 1997 issue of *National Geographic Traveler*, to Stockholmers, "the archipelago is more than an accident of geology; it is an accessory of life itself, a preoccupation, a passion, a place of summer pilgrimages, of spiritual restoration."

More than 50,000 homes have been built on the islands and along the shores of Stockholm's archipelago. Nearly all of these are summer homes, although 10,000 people live permanently on the islands. More than 120,000 boats are registered to the area, and each summer more than 1 million Stockholmers take to the water, preparing to spend most of their summer at a waterfront home. Even without a boat or a private summer home, the islands are constantly in use all summer. Ferries of all types leave continuously from Stockholm, and many islands boast tourist attractions, rental cottages, and hotels.

Many urban Swedes spend their summers in coastal cottages, where they enjoy water sports such as sailing and swimming.

During the summer, the sun shines for long periods of time—in Norrland, it never sets. With several weeks of vacation time, Swedes use this time to enjoy the outdoors almost continuously. Water sports take precedence, as families take to the country's more than ninety thousand lakes to swim, canoe, and sail. Tennis is also popular in Sweden, and the country has produced such notable stars as Björn Borg, Stefan Edberg, and Mats Wilander. Between them, Borg and Edberg have won the Wimbledon Tennis Championship seven times.

The Swedes are truly an active people, but their love of the outdoors does not exclude a love of culture and other indoor activities. Even holidays celebrate the outdoors and nature.

HOLIDAYS

Sweden celebrates the usual Judeo-Christian and secular holidays (like New Year's Eve and Independence), but many of the holidays unique to Sweden are based on nature and the seasons, and some have pagan origins. Walpurgis Night in the spring, Midsummer at the summer solstice, Lucia at the winter solstice, and summer crayfish parties all have their origins in naturally occurring or ancient events. The rituals and traditions that survive today in these Swedish celebrations can be traced back to the Vikings, medieval Catholics, and the German merchants from the Hanseatic League.

Walpurgis Night, on April 30, is a festival of German origin that welcomes the coming of spring. Big bonfires are lit to signal the start of merrymaking, and in Uppsala, students throw their winter caps into the river to mark the beginning of a twenty-four-hour period of song and cheer.

Midsummer is celebrated throughout Sweden on the weekend closest to the summer solstice (the longest day of the year), in late June. It is a huge celebration that goes nonstop all weekend—for even in southern Sweden there is some light all night by late June. Midsummer is celebrated with games, music, dances, parades, feasts, and a maypole— a large pole that is decorated with leaves, flowers, and streamers. People take hold of the streamers and dance around the pole in celebration.

In August, when summer vacation is nearly over and school will soon resume, Swedes hold yet another celebration. This time the party revolves around crayfish—the freshwater version of lobster. As the little crustaceans come into season, Swedes get together for music, fireworks, and feasts of boiled crayfish.

One of the biggest holidays in Sweden, however, is Christmas. Preparations for its celebration take up most of the month of December. Preparations for the Christmas smorgasbord, or buffet meal, might begin as early as December 1, when the advent calendars are brought out to mark the beginning of the Christmas season. These elaborate calendars have flaps over each day from December 1 until Christmas. Under each flap is a different picture surprise. Children and adults alike delight in checking the calendar each day to see what is under the little flap for that particular day.

On December 13, in the middle of the Christmas season, Lucia arrives. This is a day set aside to honor Saint Lucia, a young girl who lived in the Middle Ages and devoted her life to God instead of marrying. Traditionally, Lucia was celebrated with plenty of food and drink because folk tradition considered it the longest night of the year (the actual longest night of the year is later in December) and people needed

A crowd looks on as a maypole is raised in Leksand, Sweden. Participants take hold of streamers attached to the pole and dance around it to celebrate the summer solstice.

A ten-year-old Stockholm girl, dressed in white and wearing a crown of lit candles, offers coffee and pastries to her parents on St. Lucia Day.

the extra nourishment. Nowadays, the Lucia holiday begins with a daughter in the family donning a white gown and a crown of lit candles (symbolizing the coming of light) and serving the adults of the household coffee, glogg (a mulled spiced wine), and pastries in bed.

On Christmas Eve, the feasting begins around 3:00 P.M. and continues into the evening. Often, the Christmas gnome (a Swedish version of Santa Claus) makes an appearance, much to the delight of youngsters. On Christmas morning, most people attend church, then pass the rest of the day quietly with their families.

6

CULTURE FOR EVERYONE

From elaborately arranged smorgasbords to traditional handicrafts, Swedish culture has embraced and encouraged artistic creativity. Even in Viking times, craftsmen were accorded status, particularly those who produced jewelry and other artistic items. Today, Sweden exports a wide variety of artistic products, many of which are so distinct that they are immediately recognizable as Swedish.

According to the website Navigo,

> Due to its position on the map, Scandinavia was for a long time somewhat isolated from mainstream European culture. Since a vivid cultural exchange did not take place, folk art motifs and traditional handicrafts have instead influenced the development of modern design.[13]

Swedes feel cultural events should be accessible to everyone, and to that end, the government supports the arts by subsidizing public libraries, cultural magazines, museums, and theaters, as well as dance, music, visual arts, and literature organizations.

Swedes have also been very careful about preserving their heritage. There are more than three hundred national institutions around the country, including art, archaeology, cultural history, natural history, folk, and specialized museums—all likewise supported by the government.

MUSIC

Traditional Swedish folk songs and ballads evolved in the peasant society of the 1700s and 1800s. This type of music was originally designed to be sung while working and without instrumental accompaniment. Long ballads told stories, and lively folk songs made tasks seem easier to perform. Toward the end of the 1800s, musical instruments such as the fiddle and accordion were added as accompaniments to the songs.

Today, music is part of Sweden's school curriculum, and students learn to play different instruments while they are young. Swedes keep their musical heritage alive through annual music festivals held around the country. Festivals like the Music on Lake Siljian Festival attract hundreds of participants and huge audiences.

Modern Swedish music is also very popular around the world. Singing groups like ABBA and Ace of Base routinely

THE NOBEL PRIZES

Every year on December 10, the Nobel Prizes are presented in Stockholm. During a glittering ceremony hosted by the king of Sweden, the prestigious prizes are awarded for accomplishments in physics, chemistry, physiology or medicine, literature, and peace. In addition to these five original prizes, in 1968 Sveriges Bank (the Swedish national treasury) established a prize for economic science and dedicated it to the memory of Alfred Nobel.

Alfred Nobel is best known as the inventor of dynamite and as a shrewd entrepreneur who founded more than ninety companies and factories around the world. He patented 355 of his inventions, of which dynamite is the best known. In his will, he established a foundation, stipulating that the prizes be given to those people who have "conferred the greatest benefit on mankind." Each prize usually awards at least one hundred thousand dollars to the recipient. December 10 was chosen as the award date because it is Alfred Nobel's birthday.

The first Nobel Prizes were awarded in 1901. Since then, the prize has gone to a Swede nearly thirty times. Despite an overall dominance of male winners, the prize for literature has frequently been awarded to females. In the science field, Marie Curie won the award twice—the first time jointly with her husband and the second time by herself.

Alfred Nobel's profile graces the Nobel Peace Medal.

Ace of Base (pictured) is one of the Swedish pop groups to follow in the footsteps of 1970s band ABBA and attain international stardom.

topped the charts in the United States and Europe in the 1970s and 1990s, respectively.

The Sami have their own music, which is believed to be the oldest form of surviving music in Europe. It reflects their nomadic history and lifestyle and is often spontaneous, intensely personal, and emotional. Like traditional folk songs, most Sami songs are sung without instrumental accompaniment.

THE VISUAL AND DECORATIVE ARTS

In Sweden, art is part of everyday life. Most towns and cities are full of public works of art, such as sculptures and fountains. A testament to Sweden's love of art is the large number of art associations—approximately eighteen hundred—that exist throughout the country. Most of these associations are formed by art-loving employees of companies and institutions. The members get together to visit galleries and museums, sometimes even purchasing works of art to be used as lottery prizes at work-related events.

The best example of everyday art can be found in Stockholm's subway system. Dubbed the world's longest art gallery, more than half of the ninety-nine station stops are decorated with sculptures, engravings, mosaics, and paintings. More than seventy Swedish artists have contributed to the project since the subway system was built in the late 1940s.

Sweden is also known for both its glassworks and handicrafts. The Kosta and Orrefors companies are famous for their crystal vases and glasses, and in the Dalarna province, handicrafts such as the brightly painted and carved wooden Dalecarlian horse embody the handicraft tradition. Sweden's glass and handicraft industries form the basis of a booming tourist trade.

A glass blower gives a demonstration at the Kosta factory. Sweden's glass products are popular with tourists and bring in a significant amount of revenue.

THE ICE HOTEL

With the northern part of the country under snow and ice much of the year, Swedes have become very creative about what they do with it. Playing ice hockey and building snowmen is all well and good, but what about building a hotel entirely out of ice?

Eighty miles above the Arctic Circle, right in the heart of Swedish Lapland, there is just such a hotel. Every autumn, the Ice Hotel is chiseled and chainsawed from thousands of tons of ice in preparation for its December opening. The hotel stays open until it melts, usually around early June.

The hotel features forty bedrooms, a reception lobby, an art gallery, and a bar, and it is a popular destination for Swedes and tourists alike. Within the bedrooms, the beds are made out of blocks of ice covered with wooden boards. Special clothing is not necessary; the hotel provides Arctic-quality sleeping bags and any extra clothing guests may need.

The hotel is booked solid during the last week in January, when people come from all over to attend the Kiruna Snow Festival. The week-long celebration includes cultural events such as theater and art exhibitions as well as dog and reindeer races and a spectacular snow-sculpture competition.

One of the bedrooms in Sweden's Ice Hotel, a structure made entirely from ice.

DESIGN AND ARCHITECTURE

Sweden is known for its style of design and architecture, which has clean lines and is functional. This approach to design was originated by architect Erik Gunnar Asplund during the 1930 Stockholm Exposition and has since gone on to become identified as "Swedish style." In particular, Swedish furniture has become recognized around the world. Light-colored woods teamed with bright geometric-patterned fabric and simple lines are the instantly recognizable features of Swedish design. Swedish design also carries over to such functional household objects as bookshelves, bowls, tea kettles, silverware, and many other items—all of which are recognizable as Swedish by their clean lines and spare design.

Swedish architecture also follows some of the same functional principles. According to the Chalmers School of Architecture in Göteborg, "Architecture means the organizing of the world, using buildings as a primary medium, to create spaces and environments for people."[14] There are several schools of architecture and design in the country, and all of them are instrumental in developing and promoting Swedish style.

While Sweden is recognized for its functional and modern approach to design, the nation is also dedicated to preserving its architectural past. The Royal Opera House, built by Gustav III in the late 1700s, is still in use, as are many other historic buildings. Throughout the country hundreds of older buildings have been preserved, existing side by side with newer structures, while several museums are devoted to Swedish design and architecture, both past and present.

In the middle of Stockholm lies Skansen, an open-air museum and park complex that depicts Swedish life as it used to be. The park is divided into several areas that represent the various regions of Sweden. The historic buildings have been moved to the park from around the country, and the houses, farmsteads, and town quarters are staffed by people in period costume demonstrating traditional occupations and crafts. Besides depicting life as it used to be, Skansen also offers floral, herb, and rose gardens, as well as livestock and wild animal displays with elk, wolves, bears, lynx, and seals.

Throughout the year, Skansen serves as a site for festivals, concerts, Stockholm's Autumn and Winter Markets, and other cultural events.

THEATER AND FILM

Swedish theater dates back to the late 1700s when King Gustav III opened the doors of his theater to the general public. Prior to that, only the aristocracy attended the theater.

The country's most prestigious theater is still the Royal Dramatic Theater in Stockholm. Just outside Stockholm, the Court Theater at Drottningholm Palace (where the royal family lives) was also founded by King Gustav III in 1766. It is still used in the summertime for ballet and opera performances.

A number of amateur groups and touring companies exist throughout the country. In the summer, when most indoor theaters are closed, people attend open-air performances put on by both professional and amateur actors.

In 1963 the Swedish Film Institute was established in an effort to help the film industry and ensure that Swedish films would continue to be made. Additionally, the Gothenburg Film Festival is held annually and gives directors, actors, and others interested in film an opportunity to gather for lectures and movie watching.

Although Sweden is not known for its film industry, in the past fifty years several well-known actors and directors have hailed from Sweden: Ingmar Bergman is an internationally known director, and Ann-Margret is recognized as a great actress around the world and has starred in several successful American films. The late Greta Garbo and Ingrid Bergman were also recognized as great actresses during their time.

Sweden excels in children's films. Great care is put into the production of animated and nonanimated children's films, most of which are based on much-loved characters found in Swedish literature.

LITERATURE

Sweden is a literate nation, and Swedes read a lot. About 65 million books are borrowed at public libraries each year, and local government authorities maintain more than 2,000 libraries and 130 bookmobiles throughout the country.

ASTRID LINDGREN AND PIPPI LONGSTOCKING

Sweden's Astrid Lindgren is one of the most beloved children's authors in the world. Although she has written many books, she is best known for her series featuring Pippi Longstocking, a spunky little girl who lives on her own with a horse and a monkey to keep her company.

Lindgren was born in 1907 on a farm in the Småland region, where many of her books are set. As a child, she loved to read; *Anne of Green Gables* and *Pollyanna* were two of her favorites. Most of her books show these early influences: They feature a lonely, love-seeking child who spends a lot of time in her own fantasy world.

Pippi Longstocking, the original book in the series, was the second book Lindgren had ever written. She wrote it as a tenth birthday present for her daughter. Since then, it has gone on to become an international best-seller. Over the years, Lindgren has published Pippi sequels that have become best-sellers as well. *Pippi* has even been made into a number of movies.

Astrid Lindgren (right) is presented with a Swede of the Year award by Princess Victoria (left) and Linnea Roxenhielm (center), who played Pippi on stage.

DAG HAMMARSKJÖLD

In 1953, when the United Nations could not agree on a candidate for secretary general—the highest position in the organization—Dag Hammarskjöld was asked to accept the position. Coming from neutral Sweden, he was considered an acceptable compromise. On April 7, 1953, he was unanimously appointed secretary general of the United Nations, and in September 1957 he was again unanimously appointed for another five-year term.

Hammarskjöld was well suited for the position. He came from a family of noble civil servants, all of whom had served the Swedish monarchy since the seventeenth century. His father had been the prime minister of Sweden. Prior to assuming the position of secretary general, Hammarskjöld had spent his professional life working in political, academic, and governmental positions.

As secretary general, Hammarskjöld brought prominence to the newly formed United Nations. His devotion to the concept of nations working together to ensure world peace helped keep many member nations actively involved, even when many of them questioned the validity of the whole organization.

But Hammarskjöld's efforts toward world peace also earned him enemies. In the aftermath of World War II, many nations, including Great Britain, the United States, and Russia, were irritated at what they considered interference on the part of the United Nations. The Congo in Africa was a particular sore point. Hammarskjöld made four trips to the region in an effort to keep peace in Africa; meanwhile, he simultaneously tried to keep larger nations from interfering. On September 18, 1961, during his fourth trip to the Congo, Hammarskjöld's official UN plane mysteriously exploded as it was preparing to land in present-day Zambia. There were no survivors.

Around the world, heads of state and common people mourned the death of a remarkable man. For most people, he was a beacon of hope for the fulfillment of world peace. In 1961 he was posthumously awarded the Nobel Peace Prize—making him the first person to ever receive the coveted prize after death.

Swedish publishing is dominated by a few publishing houses. Much of their sales come from translating English best-sellers into Swedish, though. Even so, Sweden boasts several world-famous authors.

Playwright and novelist August Strindberg (1849–1912) began his career by working at the Royal Library in Stockholm and ended up writing more than seventy-five of his own books. Most of his books cover such themes as power, religious doubt, social problems, and the problems inherent in the relationships between men and women. Strindberg was also a talented painter. Another well-known author, Vilhelm Moberg (1898–1973), is famous for his books about Swedish emigrants settling in America. Moberg is also known for depicting the lives of farmers and soldiers in his home province of Småland.

Sweden also boasts world-famous children's authors. Selma Lagerlöf (1858–1940), a children's author, won a Nobel Prize for literature in 1909 and is still read around the world. Her most famous book, *The Wonderful Adventures of Nils,* has been translated into more than forty different languages. Astrid Lindgren is also famous around the world for her Pippi Longstocking books.

7

LOOKING AHEAD

During the 1990s the cost of maintaining Sweden's welfare state became astronomical. Sweden found itself swamped by financial debt, high taxes and inflation, an oversized government structure, increasing crime, and a stagnant economy.

As Sweden enters the twenty-first century, it is faced with the difficult challenge of redesigning its welfare state while still maintaining the high standard of living its people have come to expect.

A NEW MIDDLE WAY?

Between 1990 and 1993 Sweden experienced a deep recession, caused mostly because its goods were not as cost competitive as other nations'. Sweden was manufacturing goods, but outside of Sweden, they were not selling as well as they had in previous decades. Another contributing factor to Sweden's recession was overbuilding. A building boom in the late 1980s created more real estate than people or businesses could use, and when the newly built houses failed to sell, the resulting drop in real estate values severely affected Sweden's banks and other financial institutions. All of these economic changes forced the Swedish government to tighten its economic policies, which has not been popular with the Swedish people. To support the social services that Swedes have come to expect, taxes have remained high, yet not all Swedes have employment.

By international standards, Sweden's unemployment rate is very low, only about 8 percent. But for a nation that is used to full employment, the recession of the early 1990s instigated many political changes. People blamed the Social Democrats for these conditions and voted the party out of power in the 1991 elections.

But Sweden's productivity and industrialization still remain its strong points. In the course of the past one hundred

years, Sweden has gone from a primarily agrarian country with most of its workers engaged in agricultural labor to a highly industrialized country with an efficient labor force. Today, less than 3 percent of the workforce is employed in agriculture, yet Sweden's farm productivity is such that the nation provides more than 80 percent of its own food. This high rate of productivity is a hallmark of the Swedish labor force. If Sweden can maintain its high level of productivity while lowering its tax rates, Swedes may very well be able to "have it all."

Throughout the 1990s Sweden has been struggling to find a new "middle way." For many decades the quality of the average Swede's lifestyle has remained high and consistent. But with the changing political scene, the demise of the Social Democrats, and changing perceptions of the benefits of the welfare state, Swedes are rethinking their way of life.

Taxes remain a concern for most Swedes. Swedes pay a national income tax, a local income tax (which varies

A construction boom in the 1980s created a glut of unsold houses and sent real estate values plummeting.

POWER IN THE NEXT MILLENNIUM

Much of Sweden's industrial growth has stemmed from access to cheap power, namely hydroelectric power. Sweden has many natural resources but lacks significant coal and oil deposits. When Sweden entered the industrial age, nearly all the power used to run its manufacturing plants came from hydroelectricity.

Sweden's manufacturing output has outstripped its ability to produce its own power. Today, about 15 percent of the country's energy comes from hydroelectricity, with most of this generated from the main northern rivers. Like many other industrialized nations, a large portion of Sweden's energy requirements are now being met by imported fuel. Forty percent of Sweden's energy consumption comes from imported oil, and 7 percent comes from imported coal and coke. Almost 50 percent of Sweden's electricity is currently generated through nuclear power plants.

In 1980 an advisory referendum was passed, and the Riksdag decided that nuclear power would be phased out by the year 2010. But even with a referendum, the matter is still up for debate. Although Sweden would like to phase out nuclear power plants, it does not want to increase its reliance on imported fuels.

Sweden produces about 15 percent of its power from hydroelectric plants, like this one, on the country's many rivers.

Swedes enjoy clean cities, education, health care, and other social services that are paid for by high taxes.

between different municipalities and counties but is usually about 30 percent of total income), and a value-added tax (VAT) on most goods and services. To cover the cost of pensions, health insurance, and other social benefits, workers are taxed an additional 5 percent of their income and corporations are taxed approximately 33 percent of their earnings. During the recession of the early 1990s, the government realized that something needed to be done. The problem then, as now, is how to retain social services without astronomical taxes.

Swedes are rightly proud of the quality of life that is available to all who live in Sweden. Culture and education are available for all, and even with unemployment in the country, homelessness and poverty are virtually unheard of. Swedes remain committed to a high standard of living for everyone—it is an inherent characteristic of their heritage and existence. Swedes do not want this to change. But they would like to achieve it without the staggering tax burdens that currently exist. Today, most Swedes have never known anything but the social welfare state—it has been an automatic and accepted part of their lives. But for many Swedes, a social welfare state is something they will no longer automatically accept. In 1991 the government implemented tax reforms that were aimed at lowering tax rates while taxing more of the populace. Most employees now pay a lower amount in national income tax, and the local income tax is a fixed percentage of income. Whether Sweden can maintain its high standard of living for all, without the higher taxes of the past, remains to be seen.

A NONMILITARY PRESENCE IN A MILITARY WORLD

Although Sweden's political ideals of military neutrality and equality for all are not changing, its political parties and global presence are changing rapidly. In November 1994 a referendum was held and Sweden voted to join the European Union (EU). The EU is an organization of European countries whose members aim to promote free trade among themselves and use a common currency, the Euro. Citizens of member countries may also travel freely without passport restrictions.

Since January 1995, Sweden has been a full member of the EU. By joining the EU, Sweden has committed itself to more active involvement with its neighbors. Yet many Swedes are concerned that further involvement in European affairs will alter the country's firm commitment to neutrality and peace.

Sweden's strategic location between Russia and the North Atlantic has always made security a paramount issue with the Swedish people. A strong national defense system has always been an integral part of Sweden's security policy and its commitment to peace and military neutrality. But by joining the EU, Sweden has made a commitment to participate more fully in the affairs of Europe. So far, Sweden is manag-

NEUTRALITY DURING PEACETIME

During World Wars I and II, Sweden managed to remain neutral while other nations were swept into war or overrun by invading troops. Sweden maintained its neutrality during both wars through a combination of political will and luck.

Unlike some neutral nations, Sweden's decision to remain neutral is a de facto doctrine, not a de jure doctrine. This means that Sweden's decision to remain neutral is based on the political consensus of its people. Austria, for example, is a neutral country whose neutrality is a de jure doctrine, which means that the policy is written into the constitution.

After World War II, there was much discussion about whether Sweden should join the North Atlantic Treaty Organization (NATO). And in 1948–1949, Sweden was involved in talks about creating a Nordic defense alliance. The concept of the alliance died when both Norway and Denmark joined NATO.

To date, Swedes are strongly in favor of maintaining neutrality, the rationale being that it is easier to stay neutral during wartime if a nation has forged no alliances during peacetime. But with its de facto neutrality, this could change at any time based on the will of Sweden's populace.

ing to participate in European affairs while actively promoting democracy.

As a full member of the EU, Sweden participates in the decision-making process and can influence and contribute to the development of the European nations more effectively than it did as an isolated country. With the dramatic changes that have taken place in Eastern Europe and the Baltic region, Sweden has taken an active role in securing democracy and new security structures in the region. By participating in the Organization for Security and Cooperation in Europe and the Council of Europe, and by taking observer status in the Western European Union, Sweden is actively extending its influence within Europe.

Sweden's influence extends beyond the European community. Sweden may not be a military presence on the globe, but it is a highly respected nation that often serves as an example for other countries. Sweden's position on certain issues often determines the positions of other nations. For a nonmilitant, peace-promoting nation, Sweden is a powerful influence, and Swedes are recognizing this power. They want to use this power wisely within the global community.

CHANGES IN SWEDEN

While membership in the European Union has brought additional influence and benefits, it has also brought some problems to Sweden, among them changes in alcohol consumption.

By international standards and officially recorded figures, Sweden ranks low in alcohol consumption: twenty-seventh of the thirty-one surveyed European and Western countries. But alcohol consumption and abuse appear to be rising. In 1994 approximately 90 percent of all Swedish males consumed alcohol, compared to only 83 percent in 1990. Corresponding figures for females were 75 percent, up from 65 percent.

One way that Sweden has controlled alcohol consumption in the past is through taxation and governmental control. Systembolaget is the governmental agency that controls the sale of alcohol and operates all of the liquor outlets in Sweden. Sales are taxed based on the alcoholic content of beverages. The higher the alcohol content, the higher the tax. Consequently, the tax on a bottle of unflavored vodka is nearly 90 percent of the retail cost.

When Sweden joined the EU, Systembolaget had only one supplier: the state-owned V&S Vin & Spirit AB, which controlled the distilling, import, and export of all alcoholic beverages. In an agreement between the EU and the Swedish government, it was decided that Systembolaget would retain its right to control retail sales of alcohol within Sweden, but the V&S Vin & Spirit AB monopoly on production would be abolished, as would Systembolaget's monopoly on alcohol sales to restaurants.

No other member nations of the EU have monopolies on retail alcohol sales, but the Swedish government stated that its decision was based on health reasons. Still, other nations were not pleased, and the Swedish government was taken to court over the agreement. Ultimately, the agreement was confirmed as being compatible with European community

THE CHANGING FACE OF SWEDEN'S POPULATION

Like many industrialized countries, Sweden has a low birthrate, with only one child per couple being quite normal. Families with more than two children are not very common. The life expectancy of Swedes is also high, with men living to approximately seventy-six years of age and women living to approximately eighty-one.

Since the 1940s, particularly after World War II, more than 40 percent of Sweden's population growth has come from its influx of immigrants. Just as the immigrants contributed to Sweden's growth as an industrial and technological nation, they are contributing to Sweden's populace. The immigrants that have arrived in Sweden over the last fifty years or so are having more children than the native-born Swedes and are changing the profile of Sweden's typically homogeneous population.

Increasing numbers of immigrants have added variety to Sweden's mainly blond, blue-eyed population.

law and the Treaty of Rome, which outlines trade practices for EU member nations.

Although the Swedish government still retains some control over the sale of alcoholic beverages, since Sweden joined the EU in 1995, smuggled spirits entering the country are believed to have soared. The smuggling is primarily fueled by the enormous tax differences between Sweden and other European countries, and there is a rising concern that with Sweden's entrance into the EU, the use of taxation to control alcohol consumption will cease to be effective.

Although Sweden's stated aim is to reduce alcohol consumption by at least 25 percent by the year 2000—a goal that is in harmony with the health objectives for the European region established by the World Health Organization—it may not achieve its goal. Swedes are uncertain whether this is a by-product of EU membership.

As Sweden enters the next century, the issues of high taxes and the welfare state, global involvement, military neutrality, and public health will need to be clarified among the Swedish people, if not resolved. But if the past is any indication, Sweden will attempt to resolve all issues in a democratic manner that will take into consideration the good of its own populace as well as the world.

Facts About Sweden

Government

Official name: Kingdom of Sweden

Capital: Stockholm

Official language: Swedish

Chief of state: King

Head of government: Prime minister

Currency: Krona, a paper currency that equals 100 ore

Weights and measures: Metric system

People

Population: 8,856,798 (August 1998 estimate)

Official religion: Church of Sweden (Lutheran)

Land

Area and dimensions: Sweden comprises 173,732 square miles (449,964 sq. km.). The country is approximately 980 miles long (1,575 km.) and approximately 310 miles wide (500 km.). Sweden's coastline is approximately 4,600 miles long (7,600 km.), and it has 15,071 square miles (39,035 sq. km.) of inland bodies of water.

Bordering countries: Finland, to the east; Norway, to the west

Territorial sea limit: 12 miles (19 km.)

Average annual rainfall: 24 inches (61 cm.)

Largest lake: Vänern, which covers 2,156 square miles (5,584 sq. km.)

Lowest elevation: Sea level, along the coasts

Highest elevation: Mt. Kebnekaise, 6,926 feet (2,111 m.), in the Kölen Mountains

Notes

CHAPTER 1: A LAND OF CONTRASTS

1. Swedish Institute, "The History of Sweden," December 1996. www.si.se/.

2. Luleå University, Sweden, "A Bit of Swedish (and Scandinavic) History," 1998. www.luth.se/present/sweden/.

CHAPTER 2: A RICH AND DIVERSE HISTORY

3. John R. Hale, "The Viking Longship," *Scientific American*, February 1998. www.sciam.com/1998/0298issue/0298hale.html.

4. Hale, "The Viking Longship."

5. Eric Oxenstierna, *The World of the Norsemen,* trans. Janet Sondheimer. Cleveland: World, 1967, p. 127.

6. Oxenstierna, *The World of the Norsemen,* p. 127.

7. Oxenstierna, *The World of the Norsemen,* p. 129.

8. Quoted in Jason Hook, *The Vikings.* New York: Thomson Learning, 1993, p. 7.

CHAPTER 3: KINGS AND WARS

9. Navigo: The Shortcut to Sweden, "History: The Birth of the Swedish Nation State: Struggle for Power," 1999. http://smorgas bord.navigo.se/sweden/society/history/nation. html.

10. Navigo, "History: The Birth of the Swedish Nation State. "

11. Navigo: The Shortcut to Sweden, "History: The Swedish Great Power Period," 1999. http://smorgasbord.navigo.se/sweden/society/history/power-period.html.

CHAPTER 5: THE FACE OF SWEDEN TODAY

12. Navigo: The Shortcut to Sweden, "Education: Higher Education," 1999. http://smorgasbord.navigo.se/.

CHAPTER 6: CULTURE FOR EVERYONE

13. Navigo: The Shortcut to Sweden, "Culture: Swedish Art—Tradition and Renewal," 1999. http://smorgasbord.navigo.se/.

14. Chalmers School of Architecture, Sweden, "Architectural Design—Theory and History of Architecture," 1999. www.arch.chalmers.se.

CHRONOLOGY

789
First Viking attacks on England.

793
Viking attack on the Lindisfarne Monastery.

830
Vikings found the city of Dublin, Ireland.

850
Vikings begin settling in Russia and the eastern Baltic region.

862
The Russian city of Novgorod is founded by Rurik, a Swede.

875–900
Christianity is introduced to the Swedes by Saint Ansgar.

982
Erik the Red discovers Greenland.

986
Coast of North America is sighted by Bjarni Herjolfsson.

1003
Leif Eriksson lands in North America (nearly five hundred years prior to Christopher Columbus).

1100
End of Viking age.

1160
Assassination of Swedish king Erik IX Jedvardsson by a Danish prince.

1319
King Magnus Eriksson unites Sweden and Norway.

1362
Finland becomes a province of Sweden.

1397
Swedes, Danes, Finns, and Norwegians unite under one crown in the Union of Kalmar.

1477
The University of Uppsala is founded.

1520
The Bloodbath of Stockholm; the king of Denmark, Christian II, massacres more than eighty Swedish nobles.

1523
Gustav Vasa becomes the first hereditary Swedish king.

1556
Finland becomes a grand duchy of Sweden.

1618–1648
The Thirty Years' War.

1632
Gustavus II Adolph is killed at the Battle of Lützen.

1697
Karl XII becomes king of Sweden.

1709
The Russians defeat the Swedes in the Great Nordic War.

1741–1743
Russia and Sweden go to war; Sweden loses Finland to Russia.

1788–1790
Russia and Sweden are at war.

1809
The first Swedish constitution is adopted; Norway becomes a Swedish territory.

1810
The Swedish parliament chooses Jean-Baptiste-Jules Bernadotte (a French marshal close to Napoléon) as heir to the throne of Sweden.

1842
The Riksdag introduces compulsory education for all Swedish children.

1905
Norway becomes an independent country.

1914–1918
World War I; Sweden remains neutral.

1921
Sweden adopts universal suffrage; all citizens over the age of eighteen can vote.

1939–1945
World War II; Sweden remains neutral but aids refugees escaping from Nazis.

1971
The Riksdag becomes a one-house assembly (no longer a two-house assembly.)

1973
Carl XVI Gustaf becomes king of Sweden.

1974
Sweden revises its constitution.

1976
After forty-four years in power, the Social Democrats are defeated; the Center Party and other nonsocialist parties form a new government.

1980
The order of succession is changed, allowing the monarch's eldest child to inherit the throne regardless of gender.

1982
The Social Democrats are returned to parliamentary power.

1986
Sweden's prime minister, Olof Palme, is assassinated in Stockholm.

1991
The Social Democrats suffer their worst defeat at the polls.

1994
Sweden joins the European Union.

Suggestions for Further Reading

Elizabeth Janeway, *The Vikings.* New York: Random House, 1981. A concise account of Scandinavia's Viking past.

Joachim Joesten, *Stalwart Sweden.* New York: Doubleday, 1943. An account of Sweden's position as a neutral country in the midst of World War II; particularly interesting because it was written as a present-day account.

Stephen Keeler and Chris Fairclough, *We Live in Sweden.* New York: Bookwright, 1984. Offers personal stories from twenty-six different people—all with different occupations—who live in Sweden. An interesting look at the Swedish population.

Hazel Mary Martell, *The Vikings.* New York: New Discovery Books, 1992. Written for a younger audience, this book offers a lot of Viking information in a small space.

Works Consulted

Books

Glenda Bendure et al., *Scandinavia and Baltic Europe—on a Shoestring.* Hawthorn, Australia: Lonely Planet Publications, 1993. An interesting guide to the region.

Jules Brown and Mick Sinclair, *Scandinavia: The Rough Guide.* London: Rough Guides, 1997. Informative guide to all of Scandinavia.

Gerald Durrell, with Lee Durrell, *The Amateur Naturalist.* New York: Alfred A. Knopf, 1986. Good guidebook for budding naturalists. Also offers information on Linnaeus.

Fodor's, *Scandinavia: The Complete Guide to Denmark, Finland, Iceland, Norway, and Sweden.* New York: Fodor's Travel Publications, 1997. An informative guide to Scandinavia with many cultural facts.

Fodor's, *Sweden.* New York: Fodor's Travel Publications, 1998. An informative guide to Sweden.

Jason Hook, *The Vikings.* New York: Thomson Learning, 1993. Describes the history, religion, and daily life of Viking culture. Although written for a slightly younger audience, it provides an excellent resource.

Eric Oxenstierna, *The World of the Norsemen.* Trans. Janet Sondheimer. Cleveland: World, 1967. Written in a breezy style, this fact-filled book easily transcends its age.

Anne Pearson, *The Vikings.* New York: Viking, 1993. A large picture book filled with color overlays and fascinating facts.

Margaret Rogers and Robin Rogers, *Off the Beaten Track: Scandinavia.* Derbyshire, England: Moorland, 1992. Informative guide to Sweden's history and present.

Charlotte Rosen Svenson, *Culture Shock: Sweden.* Portland, OR: Graphic Arts Center, 1996. An informative travel guide to Sweden—past and present.

PERIODICALS

Charles N. Barnard, "City of Islands," *National Geographic Traveler,* July/August 1997.

John R. Hale, "The Viking Longship," *Scientific American,* February 1998.

Katherine Sorrell, "White Nights," *British Homes & Gardens,* Christmas/New Year 1998/1999.

INTERNET SOURCES

Chalmers School of Architecture, Sweden, "Architectural Design—Theory and History of Architecture, 1999. www. arch.chalmers.se.

Luleå University, Sweden, "A Bit of Swedish (and Scandinavic) History," 1998. www.luth.se.

———, "A Bit of Swedish Christmas Traditions: Tradition Around Christmas/present/sweden."

———, "A Bit of Swedish (and Scandinavic) History: Introduction," 1998. www.luth.se/.

———, "General Information About Sweden: Meanwhile, at Home on the Farm," 1998. www.luth.se/.

———, "General Information About Sweden: A Part of Swedish History: The Viking Age," 1998. www.luth.se/.

———, "General Information About Sweden: The Swedish Vikings," 1998. www.luth.se/.

———, "General Information About Sweden: The Vikings Go Westward," 1998. www.luth.se/.

———, "Public Holidays," 1998. www.luth.se/.

———, The Shortcut to Sweden, "Astra," 1999. http://smorgasbord.navigo.se/.

———, "Business Culture in Sweden," 1999. http://smorgasbord.navigo.se/.

———, "Culture: Absolutely Swedish—Outlining a National Character," 1999. http://smorgasbord.navigo.se/.

———, "Culture: Festivals," 1999. http://smorgasbord. navigo.se/.

———, "Culture: Food and Drink," 1999. http:// smorgasbord.navigo.se/.

———, "Culture: Language and Cultural Unity," 1999. http://smorgasbord.navigo.se/.

———, "Culture: Literature, Writers, and the Nobel Prize," 1999. http://smorgasbord.navigo.se/.

———, "Culture: Museums," 1999. http://smorgasbord. navigo.se/.

———, "Culture: Music," 1999. http://smorgasbord. navigo.se/.

———, "Culture: Religious Consensus," 1999. http:// smorgasbord.navigo.se/.

———, "Culture: A Short History of Sweden," 1999. http://smorgasbord.navigo.se/.

———, "Culture: Swedish Art—Tradition and Renewal," 1999. http://smorgasbord.navigo.se/.

———, "Culture: Swedish Film," 1999. http://smorgas-bord.navigo.se/.

———, "Culture: Theater, Opera, and Ballet," 1999. http://smorgasbord.navigo.se/.

———, "Education: Compulsory Education," 1999. http:// smorgasbord.navigo.se/.

———, "Education: Higher Education," 1999. http:// smorgasbord.navigo.se/.

———, "Education: Higher Education in Sweden: An Overview," 1999. http://smorgasbord.navigo.se/.

———, "Education: Post-Compulsory Education," 1999. http://smorgasbord.navigo.se/.

———, "Education: Pre-School Education," 1999. http://smorgasbord.navigo.se/.

———, "Electrolux," 1999. http://smorgasbord.navigo.se/.

———, "Foreign Trade," 1999. http://smorgasbord.navigo.se/.

———, "Government: Parliamentary System," 1999. http://smorgasbord.navigo.se/.

———, "History: The Birth of the Swedish Nation State: Struggle for Power," 1999. http://smorgasbord.navigo.se/sweden/society/history/nation.html.

———, "History: Democratic Reforms," 1999. http://smorgasbord.navigo.se/.

———, "History: Sweden in the Eighteenth and Nineteenth Centuries," 1999. http://smorgasbord.navigo.se/.

———, "History: The Swedish Great Power Period," 1999. http://smorgasbord.navigo.se/sweden/society/history/power-period.html.

———, "History: The Twentieth Century," 1999. http://smorgasbord.navigo.se/.

———, "History: The Vikings," 1999. http://smorgasbord.navigo.se/.

———, "Important Legislation in the Labor Market Field," 1999. http://smorgasbord.navigo.se/.

———, "Industry and Development (Economic History)," 1999. http://smorgasbord.navigo.se/.

———, "Major Branches of Industry," 1999. http://smorgasbord.navigo.se/.

———, "Major Companies," 1999. http://smorgasbord.navigo.se/.

———, "Nature—an Overview," 1999. http://smorgasbord.navigo.se/.

———, "Saab," 1999. http://smorgasbord.navigo.se/.

———, "Small Businesses in Sweden," 1999. http://smorgasbord.navigo.se/.

———, "Swedish Inventions," 1999. http://smorgasbord. navigo.se/.

———, "Volvo," 1999. http://smorgasbord.navigo.se/.

Drusie Shehan, "Astrid Lindgren," 1999. http://falcon.jmu. edu/schoollibrary/lindgren.htm.

Swedish Institute, "General Facts on Sweden," October 1997. www.si.se/.

———, "Geography of Sweden," April 1997. www.si.se/.

———, "The History of Sweden," December 1996. www.si.se/.

INDEX

PICTURE CREDITS

ABOUT THE AUTHOR

Lesley A. DuTemple is the author of many books for children and young adults, covering such topics as tigers, whales, polar bears, moose, and others. DuTemple lives on the edge of a canyon in Salt Lake City, Utah. She, her husband, and two young children share their property with a family of raccoons, a resident porcupine, several flocks of quail and songbirds, two peregrine falcons, and roaming herds of deer.